What's Next for the Startup Nation? A Blueprint for Sustainable Innovation (Second Edition)

Uri Goldberg

ISBN:150292854X
ISBN-13: 978-1502928542

Contents

Forward to 2nd edition

Two years have passed since 'What's Next for the Startup Nation?' was first published, and I've been delighted and humbled by the attention and conversations it initiated - by so many people from so many places around the world. Many engaged me in discussions on innovation and public policy that supports such growth, and these talks helped me gain some new perspectives and raised new questions.

While the basic premise of the book did not change, I saw a need to refine some of the arguments and update certain data. Specifically in two sections - on the definition of innovation and the assumptions regarding the global financial climate that appear in the second part of the book.

This edition also includes a new epilogue on the state of innovation, in the hope that this will help in furthering the discussion about what we refer to as "innovation" and how it is implemented at a company level. I believe this essay can help us gain perspective on the actions that various stakeholders need to take to further innovation to obtain sustainable growth both on a company and country level.

In a curious way, appreciation of the importance of innovation is growing today. Companies are dealing with this topic by addressing internal behaviors and practices that have limited their innovative abilities in the past. My hope is that this book will help decision-makers see more clearly their influence on the business sector and develop an appreciation for an integrated view.

Uri Goldberg

Tel-Aviv, Israel

September 2014

Forward

When I was ten, my parents took me to the Tel-Aviv Museum to see the opening of a new art exhibition. On our way back, my dad mentioned to my mom how dissatisfied he was that in order to understand and enjoy the exhibition, he was forced to follow a guide. Instead of following a guide, my dad wanted to wander around the space of the exhibition and stop at the paintings that he liked, taking his time with the artwork that spoke to him and not just paying attention to the ones dictated by the guide. He wanted to receive a proper explanation of the paintings and sculptures that he liked, but at the same time the ability to wander off and have a meaningful experience on his own.

By the time we got home he had an idea about how to solve this problem. For the next few weeks, he spent his evenings in his home office, thinking and drawing up plans. He drew the initial sketches for a new device and the electronic system that would support it. During that time, he also had a few conversations with one of his friends, and got him excited about the idea as well. The two of them began to envision a device that was the size of a mobile phone (this was 1990), that one could hold and walk with around a museum. The idea was that when you saw a piece of art that you liked, you would punch in a few numbers and receive an explanation about it.

The two assembled a small team, and soon after, a company by the name of ESPRO came to life. In two years, they arrived at the Louvre museum in Paris and introduced the world to the first digital personal guide—easyguide. The device gave viewers the ability to pick and choose what they wanted to hear and wander at their own paces. After the Louvre, they installed the system in the Van Gogh Museum in Amsterdam and from there they began to reach every prestigious museum and national heritage site in the world.

As my dad was busy building his first company, a massive flow of immigration started to arrive in Israel. From 1990–1995, the Israeli population would grow by almost fifteen percent, by new immigrants originating from the ex-Soviet Union. To accommodate this situation, the Bank of Israel said that the country would need 50 billion dollars in investment capital—the equivalent of the entire Israeli GDP of 1990—over a five-year period just to integrate the new population. During this time, net foreign direct investment barely reached 200 million dollars. Unemployment at the turn of the decade reached twelve percent and inflation levels were stable at twenty percent. Every day, Israelis were feeling the toll of the harsh economic conditions and, what is more, they were terrified of what would come after a huge increase in population.

As politicians talked of the need for a more labor-intensive manufacturing sector to accommodate the labor surplus that accompanied these new arrivals, stories of new companies, new ideas, and new innovations began to fill the airwaves. At first, the entrepreneurs featured in these stories were labeled 'dreamers.' At a time when the typical dream of a Jewish mother was to see her son become a lawyer or a doctor (or both), most people thought that becoming an entrepreneur or a 'dreamer' was a polite way of saying one would soon be checking into a mental facility. In 1990, this was not merely a misguided thought; the Jewish mother had facts to back her arguments. Although the Israeli high tech sector sales had grown from 2 to 3 billion dollars between 1985 and 1989, the number of employees in high-tech electronics had actually dropped, from almost 40,000 employees in 1984 to just over 33,000 at the end of the decade. This trend had raised understandable doubts about whether the high tech sector would ever be able to employ people in sufficient numbers to accommodate the massive Soviet immigration.

In 1992 as Israel was heading into an election, the state of the economy worsened still. Policies directed toward encouraging the development of labor-intensive industries had had little effect, and a sharp deterioration in the total deficit threatened to push Israel back to the hyperinflation levels of the 1980s.

However, policies and initiatives that were considered less significant, mostly those that were directed at encouraging entrepreneurs and venture capitals, were the ones that started slowly to bear fruit. These initiatives, which were relatively small in size, set up financial mechanisms for luring venture capital funds into Israel and create high tech incubators that would support early-stage entrepreneurs. By 1998, the result of these policies was clear. In a single year Israel was able to attract over 3 billion dollars in capital investment, most of which was foreign. This was a thirty-fold increase in a period of less than three years.

In 1998, the leading story in every news show was that of AOL's purchase of a small Israeli company, Mirabilis (the developer of ICQ), for a staggering 407 million dollars. Life in Israel changed overnight. Saying you had an idea that you'd been working on was no longer something you wanted to hide. By the end of 1998, Israel had over 3,000 startup companies, or one for every 2,000 inhabitants. One by one, some of these Israeli companies became public in stock markets around the world, and foreign corporations were acquiring twice as many companies as were going public.

At the turn of the century, the green color at every major stock exchange was glowing hard. It seemed as if Moore's law applied to the stock market in the same way it did to the history of computer hardware.

Everyone believed that green would rule the world. But then the unthinkable happened. The dot com bubble burst, large respectable companies could no longer weather the financial burden and were forced to file for bankruptcy. As in the world, the new Israeli heroes crumbled one by one and the Israeli technology giants, the role models of the Israeli entrepreneur age, followed suit.

On March 3rd, 2001, NICE, one of the first truly global high tech Israeli companies fired 220 of its employees. Two weeks later another Israeli giant, Gilat Satellites, announced that it would let go of 275 employees after the eighteen-year-old company had lost ninety percent of its value over a twelve months period. A month later in April, Comverse, the pioneer of voicemail, let go of 400 of its people, while making sure that access to the roofs of its buildings in northern Tel-Aviv were blocked so that no one could jump.

Many people called the eighteen months that followed the burst of the dot com bubble a ‘business hell.’ Every day new companies were being shut down, more people were being let go, and mere survival was considered success. Miraculously, Israel did not enter into a recession. However, growth levels became and stayed sluggish for the rest of the decade. Venture capital investment levels leveled and the rate of initial public offerings (IPOs) did not bounce back to late-1990s levels.

Still, the entrepreneur spirit of the dot com years never bowed its head. In terms of the rate of creation and survival of new companies (from 2003 to 2011), the business demographics of Israel have leveled, and an economic ecosystem that focused mainly on hard-core technology with little access to large businesses and end customers, has made Israel's main export to be - cutting edge technological startup companies.

The story of the Israeli economy is an amazing one. It's a story of the struggles and successes of brilliant and innovative people. People like my dad, who used to light up when walking into a shop or museum only to find a piece of equipment he developed in our basement long after the rest of us had gone to sleep. It is a story of the worries that people like my dad have before traveling to meet their first clients, and it's a story of the smile that simply doesn't go away after they install their first systems in their clients' site. And it's a story about the incredible pride my dad felt when he saw his daughter start her own company and experienced the same feelings. The story of the Israeli economy is one that is told in our house, and it is multiplied by thousands throughout the country. Yet this story is far from over. Its next chapter has yet to be written; its plot has thickened and the suspense is growing as we see new challenges appearing ahead.

The story of Israel is the story of people with ideas, but the companies they created cannot be attributed solely to the Israeli people and their wit. Government policies and practices wrote and determined the shape and form of this economy. It was both intended government intervention and negligent lack of intervention that transformed Israel into becoming the success story it is today. It was these practices that determined and forced Israelis to focus their entrepreneurial spirit on specific areas. And it will be government policies that will determine the form of the next chapter in the Israeli economic story.

*

This book is based on research and work conducted both by myself and by my colleagues while consulting and working with governments and companies across multiple industries. All of this research as well as my own work in the past has emphasized the place of innovation as a driver for growth and the central role that governments have in fostering innovation. Government policies determine both the quantity and quality of the innovation that is created by individual companies. It is also important to note that, when we talk about innovation, we are not limiting ourselves to new products but rather to every kind of innovation, from the introduction of new processes, designs, and business models to the creation of new products. We are also not limiting our discussion to entrepreneurship. Innovation does not stop after a company is created. Rather, research shows that large companies innovate more often and more successfully than their smaller companions.

The premise of this book is that, in order to support innovation, governments need to address six key questions and to support development around these key areas. These key areas are:

- *Access to capital:* To what extent and form is capital available to businesses?
- *Access to customers:* Where, of what nature, and by what quantities are customers available?
- *Access to talent:* What is the nature of available talent? What are its areas of expertise and what is its quality? To what degree is it available to businesses?
- *Access to infrastructure:* What type of infrastructure is available and what are its capabilities and capacities?
- *Access to predictable, sensible, and reliable regulation:* To what extent are regulatory changes predictable? Do they address the real needs of the society and are they being enforced equally and effectively?
- *Culture and social networks:* To what degree are people able to interact, work together, and collaborate with international networks?

An understanding of these key areas is the foundation for promoting innovation. However, these areas do need to be taken in the context of the individual state. For Israel, this context is that the world, the world in which Israeli innovation has thrived, is changing. New powers are forming and changing the very fundamentals on which our economy is based. The pace of these changes and their direction are still unknown. Faced with such uncertainties and the risks that these uncertainties entail, the only way a country can support growth and preserve its citizens' standard of living is by innovation. The aim of this book is to analyze the challenges that face the Israeli economy with respect to each of these areas. By relying on best practices as well as great failures from around the world, we will identify the main policy options that are available to the Israeli government and try to determine the impact these options may have.

*

Numerous people and institutions have given me access to their own work as well as insight into their personal and professional experiences and struggles. These people and organizations have helped me tremendously in developing my own understanding of the macroeconomic challenges, and their real life implications. Some of the individuals and organizations names that appear in this book have been altered to protect identities.

Part I- A Brief History of the Israeli Start-Up Scene

An improbable start

At the end of the 1970s, Israel was only in its early thirties. It had already endured four wars, a depression, and multiple political scandals. But hope was in the air. Peace had emerged as Israel signed its first peace agreement with an Arab country. The political landscape was showing signs of a long waited normality and to top it all, Maccabi Tel-Aviv, the national basketball team, won its first European championship. The team's forward guard, Tal Brody, proclaimed at the end of the game, "we are on the map! And we are staying on the map – not only in sports, but in everything."

Still, not all was well. Since 1970, inflation had risen steadily, from thirteen percent in 1971 to over a hundred and ten percent in 1979. In the course of the years to follow, it would reach a staggering four hundred and forty-four percent for a single year. Every day the news started its evening broadcast by reviewing the Consumer Price Index.

As the country entered the 1980s, a new crisis emerged. In the 1970s, banks had begun to manipulate their valuation as a mean of increasing capital investments. Bank stocks were considered a safe haven. People who were seeking an avenue for preserving the value of their savings would invest in bank stocks, thus driving the price of the banks' shares even higher. By early 1983, the banks were not only advising customers to buy their own stocks, they provided loans specifically designed to help people buy them. As the growth rate of these stocks began to slow, the banks attempted to preserve rates by buying back their own stocks and artificially preserving demand. Once the banks were constrained in capital, rumors started and panic broke out. Banks stocks went into a free fall. One Thursday morning in October the banks were able to absorb the supply no longer. Since the banks' equity was based mainly on their own stock prices, a full-scale banking crisis emerged. It forced the government to assume control of the four major banks at a cost of almost 7 billion dollars. Given recent financial events, this sum may seem low. At the time, however, the sum amounted to more than one quarter of Israel's GDP. By the end of the year, the public had lost over one third of its savings. A new and gloomy economic reality hit hard. People lost their life savings, their homes; unemployment rose to new highs, even divorce rates grew by eight percent.

In 1985, as the aftermath of the crisis still resonated, a new financial fear emerged. For the past five years, target revenues from tax collection were constantly not met and foreign investments were non- existent. A military operation in Lebanon was being dragged for over three years and the toll on the economy was grave. As a result government lending became constrained and interest rates soured. As the military operations were concluded, an understanding emerged that the Israeli economic structure on its various characteristics was unsustainable. Overall economic reform was overdue. The government convened all of the major economic forces and launched the '1985 Stabilization Plan'.

The Stabilization Plan marked the first time that the government took a structural approach to economic issues. It represented a paradigm shift in its thinking. Since the early days of the state of Israel, the government had viewed itself as the sole responsible entity for development. As such, it took upon itself all the major investments that were done in the country, from large construction projects through the establishment of financial institutions to running basic companies and services. This approach, along with high military expenditures, made government operation reach a staggering seventy-five percent of the economy in 1985.

The government adopted a new set of principles. These principles called for a decrease in government involvement in markets, a reduction of the state budget, and concrete steps to achieve inflation reduction to internationally acceptable levels. Although these principles were sound, creating such a transformation was difficult. A shift in financial operations and the change in the role of the government caused Israel to enter into a recession. For two years, companies went bankrupt on a daily basis, unemployment nearly doubled, and public confidence levels sank to new lows.

Gilat, Nice, and the origins of the military industrial complex

At the end of 1986, Yoel Gat was a thirty-four-year-old, well-respected officer in the Israeli Intelligence Corps.

He had led some of the corps' most complicated and sensitive development projects, which involved hundreds of developers and multi-million dollar budgets. Yet on one afternoon in November, he lost a standoff over both the leadership of his unit and the survival of his own development project. After a meeting with his superiors, he felt that his entire world had crumbled. He had been serving in the military for his entire adult life and didn't know how to operate in any other environment. No one would show him the door out of military life, but at the same time no one would try to stop him from leaving.

Some people take office supplies when they leave their jobs; Yoel took with him two of his men and one of his superior officers. Together, they were ready to change the world.

They decided to meet every evening at someone else's apartment. There they debated technology and business until the early morning, and realized that the only thing separating them from greatness was the simple realization that they had no idea what they were going to do. After a few weeks, the basic need for income began to overshadow the greatness that they expected to achieve. To overcome their financial worries, the men began to offer their services to a company that was bidding for a license to deploy cable television. They would provide everything from technical design for the project to financial and deployment management for the company.

As they calculated how to place cables underground, they never abandoned their passion for the stars. During their military service, they had been engaged in several projects that involved military applications for satellite communication. Now, when the basic need for income had been addressed by their work for the cable operator, they began to revisit their past work and to think of civilian applications for their military skills and technological know-how. Through a friend, Yoel was introduced to an executive at SpaceNet, a subsidiary of GTE (former General Telephone & Electronics Corporation, the largest independent telephone company during the days of Bell system). During a series of meetings, Yoel promised—without fully understanding how—that he would show the Virginia-based company an innovative solution to their current communication hurdles. The solution involved a small satellite dish that had the same capabilities as the larger ones that SpaceNet was currently using.

Yoel went back to Israel and registered a new company by the name of Gilat. He rented office space in the form of a small two-bedroom apartment in Tel-Aviv. At the time, the company had five registered full-time employees and a series of consultants and friends who would knock on the door at every hour of the day. After a few weeks, the police were ready to raid the apartment after the neighbors, suspicious because of the constant traffic of young men, felt certain that Yoel was running a brothel. After a few months of banging around ideas and equipment, the men were able to produce Yoel's promise to SpaceNet—a one-way satellite communication dish no larger than one meter in diameter.

The relationship with SpaceNet grew and together the Israeli and American companies were able to produce a small two-way satellite communication dish. The new product was designed mainly for large, geographically scattered retail companies, allowing communication and financial transactions from remote locations. In six years, Gilat was providing communication solutions to British Telecom, RiteAid (a large US based drug store chain), and many other large international firms. In 1993, it was ready to go public on the NASDAQ stock exchange with a valuation of over 100 million dollars. At that time, the Gilat offering was the largest initial public offering (IPO) ever of an Israeli company.

Only a year later, another Israeli company set another record. As Yoel and his team left to form Gilat, a second group from the same unit quit the military and named themselves Neptune Intelligence Computer Engineering, which in a matter of weeks became NICE. The group initially worked as subcontractors for the men and women in uniform, revenues it generated from these services were directed to the development of a telephone voice recording system. This development, which would eventually become NICE's flagship product, allowed service providers to accept telephone transactions. This was important because new government regulations required that telephone commands, with financial implications, be recorded and stored. Parts of this development, concerned with the development of a communication diagnostic tool, led to the establishment of a subsidiary – NICECom. NICECom hit the headlines in 1994 when it was sold to 3Com for 54 million dollars. It was the first major sale of an Israeli startup to a foreign company. Two years after this sale, NICE went public and went on a purchasing spree of its own, making it one of Israel's most successful companies at the time.

NICE and Gilat were both established by alumni of the Israeli intelligence corps. They all left the military at about the same time from a unit whose four-digit identification code, 8200, would become synonymous with innovation and entrepreneurship. For the next decade, these companies would serve as reminders of the potential of Israeli business and its ability to compete in the global sphere. But the ground for their success had been in the making for three decades before Gilat, NICE, and all the companies that followed came into existence and established themselves as a major part of the NASDAQ.

The origin of the Israeli technological boom can be traced to the second half of the 1960s. From the time of

Israel's independence until 1966, France was one of Israel's closest allies. The relationship was based on common interests and common enemies - Pan-Arab nationalism. The two countries closely coordinated their actions, exchanged technological know-how and even waged war together in 1956 to secure the safe passage of ships through the Suez Canal, and up until the early 1960s, France was Israel's main supplier of weapons. However, in 1962, after the election of Charles de Gaulle the relationship between the two nations started to deteriorate. Two years after de Gaulle came to power, France withdrew from Algeria and began to establish closer ties with members of the Arab League. After the Six Days War in 1967, relations with de Gaulle's government, already sensitive, deteriorated to new lows as France limited its exports of weapons to the region. In 1968, after an Israeli raid on the Beirut airport that was carried within the context of an operation against the Palestine Liberation Organization (PLO), de Gaulle declared an immediate and full weapons embargo that included weapons that Israel had already purchased and paid for in full (including fifty Mirage IIIC jets and five class 3 missile boats).

The sudden embargo forced Israel to adopt a new policy of self-reliance. This policy entailed two major elements. First, Israel would obtain the capability to develop all of the military equipment that it needed for its defense. Second, Israel would develop and deploy its own intelligence-gathering. That is, Israel would no longer rely on other nations for weapons supply or for information in defending itself. This new doctrine led to massive public investments. A combination of intelligence and R&D led to massive investments into the Intelligence Signal Corp, also known as Unit 8200. In the field of military equipment, Israel began to invest heavily in the creation of an advanced military industrial complex. In 1980, this complex took upon itself the task of developing one of its most ambitious projects yet - the creation of a world-class fighter jet, the Lavi.

The development of the Lavi fighter jet began at the end of 1982. The fighter's design was a combination of small structure and a sophisticated software system that would control all aspects of the craft's operation. Its aerodynamic design relied on the concept of 'natural instability in flight,' which, with a sophisticated control system, provided a superior flight performance. The fighter was able to carry large payloads at high speeds across long distances and deploy advanced weapons systems in case it engages in air-to-air combat. In its characteristics and performance, it was compared to the US-made F-16 and F-18 planes of the time.

In August 1987, under pressure from the Reagan administration and an understanding that the project would have devoured Israel's defense budget as well as a disproportionate share of American military aid, the Israeli government was forced to abandon the project after the creation of three prototypes and preparations for large scale manufacturing. The decision was a hard one to make and is debated still today. It was considered not only a stab to the heart of national pride but also a loss of future defense capabilities. In a 2010 editorial, Moshe Arenas, who had served as Minister of Defense on three separate occasions, wrote about the project with regret. "Just imagine Israel's position today," he wrote, "had the Lavi project not been canceled.... Much of Israel's industry would have moved a great step ahead, Israel Aerospace Industries would have become a leading developer of fighter aircraft."

Beside the national pride and loss in technological developments, the project's cancelation had horrific implications for the over 5,000 people who worked on the jet and would be let go during a severe financial recession. Some of these employees said that the project had made tremendous technological advancements, yet they feared that they would now have to leave Israel. "For people like us," one man said, "the alternative employment they will offer us here is not on our level." Only an extremely small fraction followed up on this threat. As the economic recovery began, these people would fill the ranks of many new companies and utilize their newfound technical knowledge, skills, and developments in a variety of new projects.

Cultivating the innovative fire: immigration and venture capital

Gilat and NICE ignited the fire that fueled Israel's entry into one of its most prosperous eras. Yet just as fire needs oxygen to continue to burn, so did this wildfire of innovation need its own elements in order to spread. Two things allowed Israel to enter the twenty-first century as a leader in the digital age—the immigration that followed the collapse of the Soviet Union and the rise of the Israeli venture capital industry.

*

In the biblical story, Moses turns to Pharaoh and pleads, 'Let my people go.' The biblical plea has stayed with the Jewish people ever since. It was repeated by Jewish leaders to the Ottoman sultan, to the British government to allow Jewish immigration to Israel during the first part of the twentieth century, and later towards Soviet leaders who had imprisoned Jews actively seeking to emigrate to Israel.

In October 1989, after the fall of the Soviet Union, thousands lined up in front of the Dutch embassy, which housed the Israeli delegation in Moscow. In the year to follow, over one hundred and eighty thousand people who waited in those lines arrived in Israel, increasing the country's population by four percent in just one year. The massive, continuous flow of immigration posed unprecedented challenges to the Jewish state. The government was forced to come up with housing solutions during a time in which the construction sector was nearly frozen. Ariel Sharon, then Minister of

Housing, told municipalities to "place caravans on rooftops and in courtyards."

A second challenge was finding employment for a group of people that, by the end of the decade, would account for thirteen percent of the entire working population. Up until this point, the Israeli government focused mostly on promoting labor-intensive industries, as technological industries did not prove capable of absorbing large quantities of people. Yet the new population was exceptionally well educated, not to mention over-qualified for work in such industries. Almost half of the new arrivals had university degrees, and eleven percent were engineers by training— this population more than doubled the number of available engineers in the country.

To find employment solutions for these immigrants, the government started a variety of different projects, some aimed at incentivizing employers to hire by means of grants and tax breaks and others that provided professional trainings and other services that would support entrepreneurship. One underfunded project would turn out to be the silver lining of its era. In 1990, the government diverted less than half a million dollars to the creation of four technological incubators. The model, based on an American effort of the 1960s, established four centers in which scientists would be able to develop their ideas by means of access to equipment and office space. In addition, the incubators attempted to provide managerial and business support that would allow new companies to market their developments.

In its first three years of operation, no company was able to mature and exit the incubator with a viable product. In 1993, a few months after the establishment of a new government, the Ministry of Industry, Trade and Employment conducted a review to understand the lack of success of the various projects that had been aimed at supporting entrepreneurship. The review concluded that underfunding of the project and a lack of experience on the part of the managers of the incubators had given the project little chance of succeeding.

The Israeli government decided to take a holistic approach to entrepreneurship by addressing not only early stage funding but funding throughout the entire life cycle of an early stage company's development, as well as to accompany these measures with professional assistance in the fields of management and marketing. At first, it would invest in incubators, and it would better fund, staff, and spread them throughout the country. Within five years, some thirty incubators would operate in Israel, providing startup companies with a supporting environment and salaries for the companies' founders. Second, the government increased R&D funding through the office of the Chief Scientist. This program provides guaranteed loans aimed at financing development in R&D. These loans, which were on average 150,000 to 250,000 dollars were provided as matches for private investments and repaid with interest only when a company generated revenues that have resulted from the funded R&D development. Apart from financing, the program also provides a seal of approval. Since investors are likely to lack sufficient technological knowledge that would help them evaluate technological development, the government does it for them. Independent professionals, usually academic experts within the field of the company's development, evaluate the programs as part of the approval process. An evaluator will visit the company in their offices and spend between one and two full days reviewing the company's development, engaging the R&D team, and providing his opinions about the viability of the project's prospects.

Finally, and perhaps the most significant development that the government took, was the creation of Yozma. Yozma was a 100 million dollar, partly government owned, venture capital fund. It relied on an American model but had its own unique Israeli characteristics. First, it referred to international, external experience. At the time of its foundation, Israel, although blessed with engineers, desperately needed venture capitalists. The need for international experience in order to develop sustainable companies was highlighted in the government's earlier programs. One study found that, in some sixty percent of the projects that were supported by government programs, entrepreneurs were able to reach their technical objectives yet at the same time failed to reach their marketing objectives. Yozma was designed to attract foreign investors that would provide not only funding but also international experience and connections. The fund was set up in a way that provided foreign investors with a matching fund at a rate of two to one. For every dollar a foreign investor committed to an Israeli entrepreneur, the government would commit two. Furthermore, the government provided an added incentive by giving investors the right to buy out the government's share of the fund after five years. Finally, the fund had an expiration date. By design, government involvement was limited. After five years, the government committed to evaluate its involvement within the fund and auction off its shares.

The program delivered above and beyond all expectations. Ten groups participated in the program, which together managed some 3 billion dollars. All of the participants in the original funds expanded their involvement in the country by opening new, independent venture capital funds (such as Gemini and Walden). The groups' performance attracted further groups to open or participate in funds in Israel. Within five years of the initial launch of Yozma, some sixty groups of venture capitals were active in the country, managing over 10 billion dollars in investments.

The awakening

The late 1990s were exhilarating times. Israeli companies were announcing new innovations, new products, and new ways of thinking on a daily basis. In 1997, the country's new pop culture heroes were a group of four friends who looked more like Metallica fans than entrepreneurs. These four men were the founders of Mirabilis, the creator of ICQ. Mirabilis was never meant to become a 'real business.' It was a company whose sole purpose was to be a place for 'fun and insanities,' as Amnon Amir, one of its three original founders, described it. Mirabilis was sold to AOL for a staggering 407 million dollars in cash, making it the largest purchase of an Israeli company until that time.

Other Israeli companies were building their own futures and removing inhibiting barriers. Gilat, which had been the first major Israeli IPO of the nineties, was ready to take its next big step towards becoming the biggest satellite communications company in the world. In 1999, the company announced the creation of Starband, a new service that pushed broadband, satellite-based communication onto the mass market. The new initiative would be conducted as a joint venture with Microsoft and would aim to deploy a satellite communication network to over two million household customers in just two years. As the new venture started to deploy its systems, it hit headlines all over the world as rural areas were, for the first time, able to connect to the Internet for a monthly fee. In February 2000, Gilat's stock price reached over ten times its initial price of 1993. To increase the pace of deployment, it was decided that the venture would become jointly owned by Gilat and Microsoft and would go public in November that year. Preparations were on the way for one of the most anticipated IPOs of the year.

And then there were ten days in March 2000, from Friday the 10th, when the technology NASDAQ index peaked to 5,048.62 points, doubling its value from just a year before, to March 20th, when the financial magazine Barron ran an article titled "Burning up, Warning: Internet companies are running out of cash fast." The article announced that, "for scores of new startups, that unpleasant sound is likely to be heard before the end of this year. Starved for cash, many of these companies will try to raise fresh funds by issuing more stocks or bonds, but a lot of them won't succeed." By April, a new session came into being and the world, which only a few weeks ago had been filled with joy, seemed to conclude that the stars were just too far away.

At this time, Gilat and Starband were deploying like crazy. The service was long anticipated and was well received, yet with every new installation, the company was losing money. As revenues were expected to derive from monthly subscriptions, the company waited desperately for financing. No such financing was coming. On March 11, 2001, Gilat announced for the first time that it would register a loss. The stock went into an immediate free fall; in less than a day the stock erased eight years of value. The company was thrown into what its CEO later referred to as a 'spiral of death,' and it was forced to restructure and let go of one fifth of its employees. The company's restructuring effort had little effect on the company's performance and questions began to rise about how it would be able to pay back bonds it had issued just a few years ago. By November, its stock fell to one quarter of its initial public offering price in 1993. The company, which had been the model of Israel innovation, was fighting for its survival. Outside its offices near Tel-Aviv, so was the rest of the Israeli economy.

The aftermath

Looking back, the crisis didn't hit Israel as hard as it did other places. The stories of young, promising companies shutting down and letting its people go are heart breaking. When looking at the economic data, however, the story is not as devastating as it seemed to the people who saw their dreams collapse.

The NASDAQ meltdown put a damper on the stellar performance of the country's high tech cluster, although Israel's NASDAQ companies had declined far less than the overall world average. But the market correction had also unmasked a fundamental reality. This reality was that Israeli companies were not integrated into a broad global investor base. Rather, Israel was heavily and exclusively relaying on US based investment. During the 1990s, these investments, which were mostly in R&D, grew on an annual basis of twelve percent per year. They peaked in 2000 which allowed a twenty-four percent growth in investments in R&D. These investments reached over 5 billion dollars within the private sector alone (total investments reached 21 billion dollars). As the US economy shifted, so did its investments in Israel. Over the past decade, the average growth of R&D investments has declined to a mere two percent, with negative growth in 2009.

Part II – Now what?

A new reality

By the end of the twentieth century, Israel was second only to Canada in the number of companies traded on the NASDAQ. It was second to none in the number of startup companies per capita. The companies that were established and operated within Israel attracted more venture capital dollar per capita than in any other country in the world (and they were third in the world in absolute terms). Venture capital was drawn to invest in these new technologies, new ideas, and new applications that were being created at a rate of over 50 new companies per day. Israel was nicknamed 'the land of milk and start-ups' (*The Economist*), 'The Startup Nation' (Dan Senor and Saul Singer), and 'Silicon Wadi' (playing on the Arabic word for valley).

The rise of Israeli technology companies and their participation on the global stage was a result of unique characteristics and events that took place in the twenty years that proceeded the turn of the century. As I have been describing, the massive immigration that followed the fall of the Soviet Union expanded the country's population by over twenty percent within a less than a five-year period. The immigrants that came to Israel were highly skilled, exceptionally educated, and eager to succeed in their new country. A series of government initiatives encouraged the US venture capital industry to expand their operations within the country. A newly liberated telecom industry, with massive military investment behind it, led to the development of cutting edge technologies and applications. And a series of trade agreements allowed Israeli companies to compete in US and European markets. All of these events and government policies helped to develop and shape Israeli industry in a unique way. Today, Israel technology has become the gold standard for innovation and excellence in the fields of communication, software, and security. The characteristics of today's Israeli economy, its innovative solutions, its reliance on Intellectual Property (IP) creations, and its entrepreneurial and global reach is very much the result of these events and the environment in which Israeli companies and its people grew up and operate in.

While Israel transformed into the 'Startup Nation,' other economies developed in different ways. During the 1990s, India underwent a series of reforms and investments in infrastructure. Although still considered lacking in the development of electricity, water, roads, and rail infrastructure, all of these areas were heavily invested in. During the Internet bubble that led up to 2000, heavy investments in undersea fiber optic cables connected Asia to the rest of the world. The fall that followed the economic boom resulted in the auction of cheap fiber optic cables at one-tenth of their original price, which in turn led to widely available low-cost communications infrastructure. All of these investments and events, not to mention a swell of available talent, resulted in India becoming almost overnight the center for outsourcing. The country began to host everything from call centers to basic R&D activities, and during the decade that followed, the Indian economy grew at admirable two-digit rates. Yet the engines of the Indian economy geared down after some time. Investments in infrastructure there have declined, reforms have stopped, and red-tape-bureaucracy has returned. High inflation combined with a new shortage of talent has resulted in a salary hike that reduced the country's main source of competitive advantage. Ten years later, foreign direct investments are halved (as of 2011) and the country's GDP growth rate has dropped by thirty percent (1990–2000 compared to 2000–2010).

Like India, the engines that drove Israeli economic growth could not work forever and could not increase their overall output. Despite continuing startup activity, Israel has yet to produce the giants of Silicon Valley. Companies on the scale of Apple, Google, Cisco, AMD, and Intel have not emerged from the Israeli Silicon Wadi, nor have companies half their size. Israel has also not been able to duplicate the success of its communication and security sectors in other industries and sectors. Despite investments in biotechnology, nanotechnology, and other industries, there has yet to emerge an industry with the same success characteristics as the ones that drove the Israeli success of the late 1990s.

Most countries around the world would trade for Israel's economic structure, innovation, and entrepreneurial spirit in a heartbeat. Yet not being able to reproduce its success across industries and not being able to transform companies into large, sustainable ones has taken a heavy economic toll. Small companies may have a reputation for being quicker to react to events and more innovative, but this reputation has little basis in reality and no economic data to support it. By comparison, large companies generally enjoy higher productivity and create more IP. They enjoy 'economy of scale' and for that reason are able to produce more products per dollar spent. In Europe, manufacturing companies with 250 or more workers are 30–40% more productive (per employee) than 'micro' firms with fewer than ten employees. Size also creates more room for innovation. Large companies that have developed a collaborative environment are able to encourage innovation, which generally emerges at the intersections of functions and disciplines. In addition large companies that sustain innovative cultures provide their employees more resources to try out new things and are also more tolerant of failures, which is another big part of innovation. Innovation is not about one great idea, but rather lots of bad ideas to experiment with and learn from. Big companies are able to commit to the investments that are necessary for innovation and to go through processes of trial-and-error. Big companies are able to tackle big problems. It is easier for an engineer at a large multinational to devote himself completely to a problem when he isn't also being asked to help fix the CEO's computer. In addition to being more productive and innovative, large companies offer better wages and create more jobs. The opposite notion that startup companies create more jobs has little statistical support. While it is true that a new company creates new jobs, mostly because it didn't exist before, statistical data show that, after one year, larger companies create more jobs and at a faster rate than smaller ones.

The demographic characteristics of a nation's businesses are of utmost important for its economy. The recent financial crisis has demonstrated that economies based on small and micro businesses are less resilient to external shocks. In countries such as Greece, Spain, Portugal, and Ireland, the lack of resilience of these companies created a domino effect that has led to a long and painful recovery.

Despite this economic data, policymakers worldwide have developed a fixation on small companies. Today a large part of policymakers' initiatives are geared toward supporting such companies. The lesson from the last two decades of economic downturn is that what matters most is economic growth, regardless of size. Growth matters because it enables resilience in the event of economic shock.

*

The direction in which an economy is headed, and the economic characteristics of a country depend mostly on its government and the stature of its political leaders. One of the major problems with the capitalist system is that politicians often have a hard time finding their places within it. Although we are now living in different times, a large part of the political leadership that is active today was raised under President Reagan's notion of the role of government and business. As he put it, "The nine most terrifying words in the English language are: 'I'm from the government and I'm here to help' (August 12, 1986)." Political leaders brought up in such an environment may find it hard to understand their proper role in government. Regardless of one's political position, most should agree to the notion that governments should develop, adjust, monitor, and re-develop the frameworks that set the environment for other players (e.g., for-profit organizations) to develop and prosper. They should interfere at times, and they should intervene when things are getting out of control. However, the focus of their actions should be on the boundaries and conditions that would best allow economic players to access what they need. They should adjust the environment to best suit the players within their borders, and monitor the climate in order to understand where and when investments are needed and to re-develop new frameworks, hopefully before the old ones become irrelevant and crises emerge. All of this work should be carried out with one aim in mind—improving citizens' quality of life.

The reason both the Indian and the Israeli economies slowed is because the policies that originally nourished these economies, the policies that allowed them to evolve, did not evolve with the systems that they created. These economies changed both because of their own internal growth and because of external factors and challenges that they faced. Looking forward, policies that support growth should focus on providing businesses with tools that will allow companies within their sphere to operate, innovate, and compete in an ever-evolving and ever-changing world.

An unpredictable future

There are three main changes in our economic environment that are the basis for the challenges that economies and the companies within them will face in the coming decades. These changes will likely affect the very nature of the economic structures of many countries and thus the strategies and organizational structures that companies will need to take in order to compete and operate in the new global economy. These changes will have different effects on different countries. As different countries address these changes in different ways, the balance of power between the countries will likely shift as well. These three major changes will occur in the areas of demographics, resources, and technology.

In the US and parts of Europe, the largest generation is about to retire. The retirement of the baby boomers will pose economic challenges that have never been experienced before. Apart from the decline of available workers, two additional challenges related to aging populations will put stress on the fundamentals of these countries' economic structures. The first challenge is the likelihood that the economy will experience a scarcity of capital. Older people tend to save less than others groups in society. A decline in savings reduces, in turn, the amount of available capital for investments throughout the economy (e.g., investments made by pension funds). The second challenge this demographic change will create is an increased pressure on public services. Since older people consume more public services, such as healthcare and social security, government resources will be under unprecedented pressures. As a result of these pressures, governments will be forced to raise taxes at the same time that they lower the investments and services they provide elsewhere.

The second change that will challenge economies is the availability of resources. Rising demands for natural resources such as water, oil, and land raise concerns that these resources are hitting their natural limits. As a result, the prices of these resources increase. Ever increasing commodity prices hamper companies' ability to deliver services at reduced prices. Furthermore, the limits of these resources are increasingly creating gaps between supply and demand. These gaps may affect not only the competitive nature of different companies, but overall social stability as well, which is the main basis for all economic development. Numerous reports, mainly from UN and the World Bank, quantify these gaps:

- Demand for food will increase by 50% by 2030 (or 3% per year), while food yields are growing at only 1.1% per year. Current rises in outputs are constrained further due to a decline in crops used for food. As energy prices rise, agricultural land is increasingly used for crops that can be transformed into ethanol. The effects of this process were clearly seen between 2006 and 2008 as the average world prices of rice rose by 217%, wheat by 136%, corn by 125%, and soybeans by 107%. In April 2008, food prices peaked to an all-time high when rice prices more than doubled in just four months. World riots followed soon throughout developing nations.
- Current rates of water extraction are unsustainable. 1.2 billion people live in conditions

where the physical scarcity of water is absolute. Current projections suggest that by 2025, 1.8 billion people will live in water-stressed conditions.

- The International Energy Agency claims that development in new oil production has fallen sharply, mostly because of the higher risks that are involved in new processes of extraction. From 2005 to 2010, crude oil prices doubled from 50 dollars per barrel of crude oil to over 100 dollars (2010, year average).
- Environmental changes accompanied by large-scale urbanization reduce the availability of land and increase its overall price.

These two fundamental alterations—demographic changes and limited resources—are accompanied by a third fundamental change. This change is the creation of new technologies and the progression of science. We can try to predict and model the effects and challenges of the first two factors, but the changes caused by technology development are harder to predict. Just imagine the changes caused by the mobile phone, the personal computer, or the washing machine. Each of these basic changes produced productivity gains, new economic sectors and industries, and each changed the basic ways in which we work, communicate, and live.

Understanding these changes is important, but is not enough. Addressing them in ways that will allow countries and their economies to gain momentum in a positive direction is the real challenge. Our leaders need to address these challenges in an ongoing way, a way in which all parties understand that there is no one time investment that will end the outcomes of these changes, and that reforms will need to be updated regularly. When President Roosevelt established the Social Security system in 1935, he understood that the system would need to be amended over time. He understood that the population structure over which he presided was likely to change. He could not however, predict the direction in which these changes would take place. He could not predict the sudden rise of pregnancies at the end of a world war that had yet to start, nor the declining rate of birth in the decades to follow. Knowing that he could not foresee all eventualities, he created a system in the hope that, when change was needed, the system would be amended accordingly. Sadly, just as he could not predict the war that would start in only four years' time, he could not predict the inability of future politicians to amend the system in order to address present day challenges.

The ability to instigate constant changes as new conditions materialize is not easy. Change requires effort, which in Western economies requires both the political will and the political capital. The ability of governments to raise this political capital in order to make these changes is limited to times of crisis. The shrinking of Japan's population, which has occurred for over two decades, and the challenges it presents to its economy, is one such example of an inability to act. As economic growth is highly correlated with population growth (on average, demographics alone account for 60% of economic growth), the economy of Japan is likely to face an unprecedented 'productivity challenge' that will require an over fifty percent increase in productivity solely to maintain the country's historic levels of economic activity. These levels will not allow Japan to grow at the rates it did in the 1970s or 1980s, but only to maintain its current levels of quality of life and zero percent growth. Despite this reality, the

Japanese government has yet to take action, such as revisions to the country's immigration policies or labor reforms needed to allow Japanese companies to operate in a shrinking economy.

Just as is the case in Japan, the governments of many countries are not able to act until crises emerge. Many wait for a 'sputnik moment,' an event that would be so profound that will serve as a wake-up call and lead to necessary reforms. The unfortunate truth is that the challenges that countries now face are not ones that will sneak up on them, but might be better illustrated as a rolling snow-ball that as time goes by becomes ever more great, ever more complex, and ever more damaging.

We must accept that the fundamentals on which our economy is based are shifting and will continue to do so. The notion, or hope, that we can somehow change these basic factors is unrealistic. We cannot refill oil reserves, nor expand the size of our Earth; we cannot get rid of old people (at least without attending to serious moral questions), and we cannot and should not restrict scientific and technological progress.

Depressing as it may sound, we the people and the government that we have elected need, to face up to reality, understand the forces at work, and accept them. We should also accept that these forces are not by themselves negative elements. They will not necessarily have a negative impact, although they do have the potential to cripple world economies in ways we have never seen.

We should understand these risks and opportunities and think through the proper roles that governments have to play. They must prepare the best environment for their people and companies, and they must do so knowing that they do not and cannot predict the overall direction of the economy. Former Secretary of Defense Rumsfeld may have said it best. During a press conference in 2002 regarding intelligence that linked Iraq to terror groups, he said, “There are known knowns; there are things we know we know. We also know there are known unknowns; that is to say we know there are some things we do not know. But there are also unknown unknowns—there are things we do not know we don't know.” Although Rumsfeld was talking about the limits of military intelligence, he might as well have been talking about the unknowns facing the global economy. As in military strategy, when one is faced with inconclusive intelligence, one should aim to create an environment that is flexible and inclusive to support any scenario that may materialize. In war generals need to coordinate their troops in a way that will create an environment that each type of force (e.g., infantry, armor) operates in the most efficient way to win the battle. In the war for growth, governments need to create an environment in which companies can strive and be free to grow by means of innovation, regardless of the direction the greater economy may take.

Part III - A path toward sustainable innovation

The basics

Regardless of the characteristics that a given economy may develop, the product of a healthy economy must involve a focus on innovation. It should be clear as well that innovation does not equal entrepreneurship (although some entrepreneurs are incredibly innovative), and that innovation is not limited to new products, as it should include new working methods as well. Innovating is not an easy task. It requires large quantities of resources and an environment of openness. Governments have a clear role to play by setting this environment and by that allow companies to direct their resources toward innovation. They can do this by eliminating barriers for companies (e.g., barriers of entry) and as such create the environment where business can develop and grow. Eliminating these barriers requires that government develop specific areas and maintain a healthy balance between them. The extent to which a particular development area progresses will determine the characteristics of that country, and it will influence the strategy companies take while operating in the country. The six key areas of development and the barriers they entail can be clarified by asking the following questions:

- *Access to capital:* To what extent and form is capital available for business?
- *Access to customers:* Where, of what nature and of which quantity are the customers available for businesses?
- *Access to talent:* What is the nature of the available talent. What are its expertise, its quality and to what degree is it available to businesses?
- *Access to infrastructure:* What type of infrastructure is available in a country and what are its capabilities and capacity?
- *Access to predictable, sensible and reliable regulation*: To what extent are regulatory changes predictable, address real needs of the society and are being enforced?
- *Culture and social networks:* To what degree are people able to interact and work together and collaborate with international networks?

Answering these questions and removing the barriers

associated with them can serve as a blueprint for sustainable development. The following sections are aimed at exploring these questions with an emphasis on the state of Israel and the specific challenges that Israel faces as it tries to mature within each area and help innovation flourish.

1. Access to Capital

The story of Google is usually told as a story of remarkable technology and innovation, but it can also be told in another way. The alternative story involves nerves of steel, good will, and a ton of luck. Nerves from its founders, who saw their project growing rapidly in traffic and expenses, with no income to support it. Good will from Stanford University, which was willing to allow its communication network and servers to be taken over. And a specific instance of luck that materialized in the summer of 1998. That summer, Google was about to vanish as quickly as it appeared. The yet to be founded company needed more servers and computer power in order to keep up with growing demand. In addition, the young founders had no revenue stream, nor any idea about how to find one. *Wired* magazine continues this story:

> *Their technology was solid, but not solid enough to impress either the money boys or the major Internet portals, so they continued struggling for*

> *financial support. Enter Andy Bechtolsheim, a founder of Sun Microsystems, who was one of the few to see the true potential of what Brin and Page had wrought. During their presentation to him, Bechtolsheim said he had to duck out for another meeting and offered to write them a check. It was that hundred-grander, made out to Google Inc., that got the ball (and the bank) rolling. Brin and Page incorporated, managed to attract other investors, with an initial investment of around 1 million dollars.*

Andy Bechtolsheim probably backed the not-yet-founded company out of a pure attraction to technology. It is unlikely that even he understood the potential that the search engine had as a source of future revenue. Sadly, most investors are more financially driven when looking at investment opportunities, and prudent when they view the potential of capitalizing on their investments. Yet, cautious as they may be, over the past three decades, falling interest rates have led investors to shift from traditional fixed-income instruments and deposits toward investments that involve more risk and more return. These investments include alternative investment models like private equity, hedge funds, and venture capitals.

Since the 1980s, the interest rates for borrowing money have fallen around the world, creating what some have referred to as 'cheap money.' That is to say, since the 1980s, the price of acquiring capital has been low. This low price led investors to increase risks within their portfolios, and this led to the global rise of venture capital. Three reasons are typically cited as having led to this situation. The first is the preponderance of loose monetary policies. Central banks have pushed to keep inflation at low levels and to do so they have loaned at low interest rates. Federal Reserve Chairman Ben Bernanke provided the second reason in a 2005 speech. Bernanke coined the term 'global savings glut,' which he referred to as a state in which there is far more savings than investment opportunities. The third reason, detailed in a McKinsey article of 2010, is an overall decline in capital investments. McKinsey research found that since 1980 the world has invested 20 trillion dollars less than it would have if it had continued the investment rates of the 1970s. All these forces, which are global in nature, constitute the underling causes that created low returns on traditional investments and an appetite for risk taking, and by that course, freed up money for new high risk technology based companies.

The forces that have led to low interest rates over the last few decades seem to be coming to an end. The primary reason for this is that developing countries are embarking on the largest building boom in world history. Rapid urbanization accompanied by rapid economic development is seizing massive investments in Asia, South America, and parts of Africa. These investments include water infrastructure, power grids, schools, healthcare systems, and housing. In addition to this investment boom, we are seeing the effects of demographic changes on savings. As mentioned before, aging populations display tendencies to save less. As we are seeing the retirement of the greatest generation (in number), overall savings and by that account available capital for investments, are bound to fall.

Since savings and investments balance one another by definition, a fall in savings and a rise in investments will cause the cost of capital to rise. This rise is likely to have an effect on investment strategies. Investors will rethink their holdings as an increase in interest rates could translate into losses for bondholders. In addition, this environment might lead to better returns at a lower risk. Such a situation may carve out some of the risk-taking appetite that investors currently hold. As new companies are more risky by nature, they will be the first to suffer from such a situation.

This situation will also affect existing companies, which will have to rethink their growth strategies. However, not all companies will be affected by this shift in the same way. Capital-intensive industries such as telecommunications, pharmaceuticals, and energy, all of which are categorized by large investments and slow returns, will face higher costs and more competition for funding. Companies that belong to industries such as retail, software, and manufacturing may be less affected as their business models require lower levels of investment and offer more immediate returns.

*

"Please come in." A young woman in a business suit pleaded, almost begging, a group of people that were talking in the lobby. One by one, she turned to different people, rushing them into the building's main conference hall in Airport City, a convention center near the Ben-Gurion airport in Israel. Slowly, the crowd listened and complied. People started to enter the hall and take their seats. Legions of entrepreneurs had applied for a slot to present at this conference. Ten companies were selected and each received six minutes to present their development projects. In the audience was a mixture of investors, analysts from local VCs, and other entrepreneurs who were seeking to find someone to whom they might pitch their projects.

Prior to the event, the organizers of the conference assigned a coach to each presenter. Each company practiced its presentation in front of a camcorder and refined it over the course of three evenings. Later, the presenter practiced responses to questions from investors and tried to tailor his response to each investor's preferences and way of thinking.

After a few opening remarks from the conference's sponsors, the first speaker took center stage. A slim, tall man in his mid-thirties, dressed in a dress shirt presented himself as the founder of a company named Novell. He presented a short video about his product, a platform used to combine databases that would allow companies to better manage and access their internal knowledge. Next came a presenter from GUI-Inc., who showed how the company could simulate human vision, enabling improved designs in complex technology-based instruments like helmets for fighter pilots. GUI-Inc. was followed by a software development company that was able to place virtual products in YouTube videos.

After the presentations ended, the crowd returned to the lobby where each entrepreneur tried to identify which of the people was coming from a venture capital, who might be a potential investor and to whom they can deliver their elevator speech. On average, three such events take place every week in Israel, each sponsored by a different company, venture capital, chamber of commerce, or academic institution. And the legions of young Israeli technology firms, who clamor for attention and money, jump at the opportunity to present themselves.

When looking at venture capital funds per square meter, Tel-Aviv is second in the world only to San Francisco. In 2010, in the midst of the recovery from the financial crisis, Israel was able to attract more investment per capita than any other country in the world. During this time, Europe attracted 7.5 dollars per capita, the US attracted ten times that amount—75 dollars—and Israel attracted 170 dollars per capita. This capital, however, seems to be running dry. Overall foreign direct investments in 2010 fell to half of the levels at which it was in 2000. In 2011, the vast majority of venture capital firms in Israel, just as in any other country, were not able to raise new funds. Not able to attract new investors, venture capital funds are hesitant to deploy the resources they do have in the fear that their current portfolios may need this money in the near future. Unable to raise capital, some are forced to pull out, slowly and quietly, from the Israeli startup scene.

*

Today, Israel faces two main problems with regard to financing. The first is the lack of availability of seed money to jumpstart new ventures. Due to the broad, global availability of capital and risk alternatives, venture capitals are playing a diminishing role in the Israeli high tech sector. According to the Israel Venture Capital Research Center (VCRC), venture capital funds accounted for less than a quarter of all funds raised by Israeli companies in 2011. This amount is almost half of the rate of their participation only a few years ago. The second problem facing Israeli companies is the low availability of the capital that is needed for more advanced initiatives. Those that are seeking to raise money that will allow them to pursue growth opportunities are finding capital less accessible. These two limitations are the direct result of a global appetite for risk and the strategy of restraint lending that has been taken by institutional investors and banks.

Israel has faced similar issues in the past. In the mid 1990s, faced with massive immigration and low investments, the Israeli government created Yozma, a series of funds that offered investors matching funds to their investments. By this the government-helped investors mitigate some of the risks associated with early stage investments. These types of initiatives promoted growth at a time when investors were reluctant to take risks, as alternative investments were more attractive. The Israeli government was wise to pull out of the industry once it was established and levels of investment were relatively stable. As investment levels have dropped again, the government would be wise to deploy initiatives that are similar to those it took in the 1990s. These strategies helped early-stage investors to mitigate their risk while at the same time preserve previous levels of investment.

The more difficult issue to which the government needs to attend is the low availability of larger investments that allow companies to take the next steps in their development. To facilitate such growth, companies usually rely on institutional investors (e.g., pension funds, insurance funds). These investments are possible only in a climate in which there are sufficient levels of savings. To facilitate such savings and hence create new investments, governments can help increase household savings. This can be done either by raising and mandating minimum retirement contributions or by making savings instruments more attractive (e.g., providing tax incentives). In addition to these measures, the government can also contribute to increasing investment levels by cutting its own expenditures. Persistent negative savings, as is the case with the Israeli government, not only reduces the country's overall savings and available capital for investments, but also creates the expectation of higher future taxes, thus damaging the prospect of long term investments as well as the overall competitiveness of local businesses in search of capital.

2. Access to customers

It may sound counterintuitive that governments have a role to play in providing businesses access to customers. We tend to overlook the complexity and the variety of forms that financial transactions can take. However, when examining financial transactions across the world, we find that they differ in both quantity and quality. These differences carry clear traces of government intervention. The forms that government policies take towards internal and external markets determine the forms in which businesses access their customers, just as they determine the nature of those customers and the nature of the relationships that evolve between a company and its customers.

Broadly speaking, a government can help business access customers in three different ways. The first is to become a customer itself. Globally, governments are the largest customers available to businesses. They manage billions of dollars of procurement budgets, all of which are directed at a large base of companies. The second way that governments provide access to customers is by promoting the consumption of goods and services within their own territories. And the final way they perform this vital function is by providing companies with access to new territories and markets. This last activity is conducted in the guise of foreign relations. A large portion of foreign policy activities of a country is directed towards agreements between states that promote each state's financial interests and facilitate cooperation between businesses.

Governments are usually reliable and attractive customers for businesses. On a regular basis, they buy everything from toilet paper to aircraft carriers, and require services that range from cleaning to consultancy (even consultancy about their procurement policies). As such, the impact of government activity on businesses is substantial and can be used to achieve different policy objectives. One of the reasons that governments use their position as customers is to stimulate financial activity. This notion is not new to the recent financial crisis, although the magnitude of the current stimulus activities undertaken by Western governments is unprecedented. The first case of stimulus measures was the New Deal, when the US government under President Roosevelt doubled its expenditure during the 1930s through a large variety of programs and projects. The sheer volume of these projects slashed unemployment from a twenty-four percent high to less than thirteen percent within four years, and boosted economic activity leading up to the Second World War. The importance of governments as clients is not limited to times of slow economic recovery, government activity is valuable under normal conditions as well. A good illustration of this importance can be derived from the effect of austerity measures undertaken by European governments in the aftermath of the recent financial crisis. Growing concern over deficits forced governments to cut spending. These expenditures were both non-discretionary, such as social security and healthcare, and discretionary, such as the day-to-day services and goods that governments provide to their people. Cutbacks in these activities resulted in reduced purchasing. Countries like Greece were hit the hardest at this time not only because of the amount of debt they possessed, but also because of business demographics. The Greek economy is composed mostly of micro-companies that employ less than ten employees. For many of these companies, the Greek government was their main client. Overnight, these companies found that banks were not willing to extend their credit either because of concerns that the government would stop purchasing their services or because fears of government insolvency. The little credit that was granted to Greek businesses came with high interest rates, as local companies were not able to assure banks that they would be paid for services delivered, or whether the expected payments would be delivered on time.

Governments have been using their powers as clients not only to deliver services, but also as a means of preserving social norms and delivering social benefits to their people. The Saudi government, for example, is criticized for using its power to preserve some of the social structures, customs, and behaviors of the kingdom. The Saudi economy is an economy in which large segments of the population cannot actively participate in business activities. The main group absent from the Saudi economy is women. Women are absent both from the workforce and from the market place, as consumers. A series of reforms have raised the participation of women in the workforce from just three percent in 1980 to over ten percent today, yet these rates are still the lowest among all Arab countries. By actively over-participating in the economy, the Saudi government is able to use its over 50 billion dollars of oil-generated revenue for providing services and goods to its population. Hence, the population enjoys a substitute for its own activities and is not obliged to participate in economic activity.

Understanding the power of governments as clients and the ways in which economies can be built around this power can provide us with insights into the implications of such activities, both positive and negative, on business competitiveness. The Chinese economy serves as a good case study. China has been slowly yet steadily lowering its government's role in the economy since the late 1970s. At the beginning of the 1990s, most Chinese companies were still government-owned. The government determined production and marketing plans for its companies, aiming to secure the services and products that it needed. These products and services are worth over 1.7 trillion dollars. To deliver to such a large client, Chinese enterprises had to develop in both size and range. By the end of the twentieth century, Western brands began to enter China. To defend their market, Chinese companies used their size, developed to serve the needs of the government, as a means of competitive advantage. Their large size operations allowed them to secure their local markets and expand into new ones. They were able to do this because of two important factors. First, they were in a position where increasing productivity was relatively easy. Due to their size and relatively cheap production costs, they were able to increase productivity by magnitudes that their Western competitors could not match. Second, they were able to raise capital and make investments, largely because they could use the government as a powerful stakeholder. Due to this economy of scale and its partly secured markets, they were able to take risks and expand beyond their own borders, offering products at lower costs than their foreign competitors.

*

Apart from becoming a client, governments can promote

consumption by its population in other means. However, creating an environment for consumption entails, in part, changes in social norms. It requires changes in behaviors, and these can be achieved in different forms. Some of these forms involve supporting the introduction or the change of elements that support economic activities like mobile communication, advanced transportation or even electricity.

Contrary to popular belief, it is unlikely that Thomas Edison invented the first revolutionary light bulb. In fact, historians have listed some twenty inventors of incandescent lamps prior to Edison's invention. The reason that Edison was successful was not his ability to create a higher vacuum within the bulb or a more conductive filament wire, but rather his ability to move a society from a dependence on kerosene to a dependence on electricity. Edison's greatness lies not in the invention of the light bulb, but in the construction of a system that combined generators, meters, and transmission lines. His ability to provide this system was in large part due to his ability to gather and receive regulatory support for his new concept. In order to operate an electrical system, standards needed to be defined, safety measures needed to be written, and regulation needed to be adjusted so as to facilitate construction and use of electricity. Such support and approval materialized in September 1882, after which Edison was able to launch the first commercial bate-site, a power plant in lower Manhattan (Pearl Street). Over a short period of time, the site evolved from a nighttime generator to a complete, twenty-four-hour facility. Edison soon expended his operations and incorporated it under the name of Edison General Electric, which became one of the most profitable companies in the world with revenues that exceed 147 billion dollars (2011), now operating under the name General Electric (GE). The light bulb would never have been able to gain customers, nor would we have seen the creation of the consumer electronics industry, without Edison's ability to change government regulation. This regulation was vital in allowing Edison to create the first electric infrastructure.

A little over a century after GE came to life, a new electric entrepreneur is seeking government's endorsement that would allow him to access customers and change the way we look at transportation. Shai

Agassi was a top executive at SAP when he decided to pursue a higher calling—building an integrated system of battery exchange and recharging stations that would support the mass deployment of electric vehicles. Agassi was able to persuade the elected officials of Australia, California, Denmark, Hawaii, Israel, and Ontario to follow this dream. These governments have started to change safety regulations, taxation, and transportation laws to be inclusive of electric vehicles. By addressing and engaging with governments, Agassi was able to reduce taxation on electric cars, making them more affordable and competitive with internal combustion engine-driven vehicles. By addressing the issue of infrastructure regulation, he was able to include his battery changing and recharging stations within a new electric infrastructure. Without these regulatory changes, Agassi would not be able to access customers and offer them a new model for their transportation and a hope of breaking our dependence on oil as an energy source.

*

The creation of infrastructures and the provision of

access to these infrastructures is a first step in ensuring companies' ability to access new customers. New Zealand is a recent example of how investments in infrastructure have supported companies' ability to access customers. The country's continued investments in its ports have transformed the remote island into an export-based economy with major trade partners throughout Asia, Europe, and the Americas. The country is a huge exporter of agriculture products and the leading exporter of dairy products. Its industrial sectors are also a huge beneficiary of the country's infrastructure investments. Due to its ability to export goods in a quick, efficient and reliable manner, alongside its highly educated workforce, leading companies are now placing factories in this remote country that are dedicated to 'hard-to-make' components. By creating an advanced, well-functioning port system, New Zealand has been able to eliminate its relative economic disadvantages of being geographically remote from major markets.

The ability to access international customers is not only the result of its advanced ports, but of its government's diplomatic activity. New Zealand is a country of just over four million inhabitants, but it employs more diplomats and trade attachés than India, which has a population of over one billion. The difference between the Indian and the New Zealand economies illustrates the significance of a country's diplomatic activity. The Indian economy has historically grown with an internal focus. The direction of India's growth resulted first from its lack of cooperation within its own neighborhood. Even today, the countries that neighbor India, despite accounting for more than a quarter of the world population, account for only half of one percent of India's imports, and they consume less than four percent of its exports.

The India example emphasizes that, despite our progress, we are still living in a world defined by man-made borders. These borders are not the simple gates through which one needs to pass, but markets with different governance systems, currencies, customs, tax regimes, and industry-specific regulations. In his 2005 bestseller book *The World is Flat*, Thomas Friedman describes a new world order. An order in which, companies and individuals can compete on a global scale. This world, as Friedman describes it, is flat in the sense that opportunities are available to all. Going global is as easy, or at least not as hard, as working and providing solely for local markets. Despite this open environment, the boundaries, although eased in some places, have been set up for centuries. Dismantling them is a long and drawn out process.

Even in today's Europe, where a series of treaties have left borders abandoned and the movement of goods and services has been greatly eased, the regulation of some industries continue to limit companies' abilities to provide services across national borders. The telecommunication industry for example, although theoretically governed by the same European rules, is still local. Telecommunication companies in Belgium do not market their mobile services to France or the Netherlands. This happens despite currency, market structures and in parts even languages that are identical. In the pharmaceutical industry, a company that wishes to market a drug on the European continent is required to submit individual applications to each country's health authority for the same drug. Again, this occurs despite the fact that these countries share common and compatible regulations.

The barriers to provide global services are still in place today. Despite amazing progress in bringing the world together on these issues, we have yet to live within a truly integrated economic zone nor a truly flat world. Accepting this fact, the role of governments should be to balance the concept of 'sovereignty' with that of 'openness.' Preserving the correct balance between these two concepts is a difficult task. Governments usually decide on the nature of this balance, while asking the question, 'Openness to whom?' This openness, that creates access for foreign companies, differs in range. From one of a limited scope, through agreements between nations on issues such as taxes, to one of complete openness. The latter situation occurs when a company does not even notice the existence of a barrier. Complete openness makes the lines on the map irrelevant to a company's activities.

Openness, or lack thereof, can be subtle or explicit. For example, at the end of 2011, the Chinese government started to place pressure on Chinese airlines to suspend or cancel EADS-Airbus jet purchases. This move came as a response to the EU's flagship Emissions Trading Scheme (ETS), which would include carbon emissions from all planes passing through European airspace. This new regulation in essence places a new carbon tax on airlines. Because of their operation methods (in terms of routes, types of aircrafts, etc.), this new tax is likely to have a disproportional effect on Chinese companies. In this case, the Chinese government deliberately raised barriers to outside companies (in this case, EADS) to prevent access to its base of customers.

The most common ways in which countries provide access to foreign companies is by economic agreements. The quality and scope of these agreements is not identical across countries but is decided on a case-to-case basis according to countries' overall relations and interests. The ability, for example, of an American company and a Brazilian company to operate and sell services in Germany is not the same. The American company is able to sell its products with no customs, under compatible tax regimes that prevent double taxation (i.e., paying taxes in both Germany and the US). It also enjoys the same access rights to the judiciary in cases of dispute, and don't need to adjust for health and environmental regulations since Germany considers US regulation as compatible to its own. By contrast, the Brazilian company needs to apply for a variety of exemptions, and it must work through numerous government departments both in Europe and Brazil to be able to sell its goods in Germany. These restrictions increase the cost of doing business, to the Brazilian company, making the company less competitive than its identical American counterpart. The ability of the American company to easily do business and access German customers is a result of a series of bilateral trade agreements that are constantly modified to serve both European and US interests.

*

In a nation of 7.6 million people, customers are a rare species. This reality has forced Israeli companies to become global from the get-go. As we saw earlier, it is the government's international activities that truly allow these companies to go global and not have to rely on a limited, local market for growth. Israeli government activities come in three forms. The first is trade agreements that are periodically negotiated, signed, and revised. The second is the government's international activity. This activity led to specific cooperation programs and frameworks. The most noteworthy of these agreements are the ones that resulted in the creation of government funds that encouraged companies to cooperate with their foreign counterparts. The third activity is the promotion of Israeli companies through conferences, events, and, in some cases, through individual assistance by using government's foreign representatives.

Historically, Israeli firms that have sought to go global have gone to the US. The ability to do so was the result of trade agreements between the two countries, the first of which was signed in 1965. This agreement allowed specific Israeli companies to sell products in US Navy ship stores. It allowed only the selling of Israeli-made products when the ships were located in non-US territorial waters. The ability of Israel to sell products in the US with relative ease was only granted in 1975. The 1975 agreement allowed Israeli companies to be semi-competitive in the US by preventing double taxation. Beforehand a company selling in the US was taxed once in the US for revenues generated from sales there and then again for income in Israel. It took another five years for an agreement that would lower economic burden further due to accounting differences. The next step in the improvement in economic relations came into effect at the end of the 1980s. Up to this point, Israeli products sold in the US had to pay customs, making Israeli products more expensive to American consumers than their domestic made counterparts. The last in this series was the 1994 agreement concerned with the mutual respect of local income taxes. This agreement allowed service companies to enjoy the same terms as goods-exporting companies, and as such were able to operate freely and effectively in the US. This progression in economic relations has since been duplicated in Europe and to some extent with other nations across the world.

The quality of the economic agreements that Israel enjoys with the US and Europe is not the norm. Europe, for instance, only has close economic ties through association agreements (treaties that create a framework for economic cooperation between the EU and non-EU countries) with fewer than thirty countries. It does have additional treaties, but these are not of the same quality. The rarity of such agreements and the significance they hold can be seen in the case of the Israeli peace process and its greater, regional relations. In 1996, in order to promote Israel's relations with Egypt and Jordan, the US Congress authorized the designation of Qualifying Industrial Zones (QIZs) between Israel and Jordan, and Israel and Egypt. These QIZs allow Egypt and Jordan to export products to the US under the same conditions that Israel enjoys (in terms of customs and taxation). To promote this progressive economic relation, this new ability was limited only to products that possess at least eight percent Israeli input within the final product.

Apart from the ability to sell goods in external markets, Israeli companies enjoy other forms of cooperation with foreign companies. These too are a result of government-negotiated agreements. The first such agreement created the Israel-US Bi-National Industrial Research and Development Foundation (BIRD Foundation). Established in 1977, the Foundation helps Israeli companies develop and go to market in the US. The foundation operates both as a financing tool and as a matchmaking service between Israeli companies with good R&D capabilities and American firms with a strong marketing backbone. To encourage these companies to cooperate, the Foundation provides funds, which finance up to fifty percent of any given product's development. Since its inception, the Foundation has approved over 800 projects that have generated over 8 billion dollars in revenue. With the success of the BIRD foundation, Israel has formed four similar initiatives (with Canada, Korea, Singapore and the UK), and is participating in other R&D programs in Europe (e.g., FP7), which help companies' access customers across the globe as well as encourage large-scale R&D activities.

*

The quality of economic relations between nations is not a finished product but one that requires constant maintenance and updating. Organizations that create R&D funds, which support collaboration, need to be constantly funded and managed. Trade agreements need to be updated periodically to reflect changes in economic conditions and to include new industries and interests that may have not been present or have evolved since the previous agreements were signed.

However, updating these agreements requires extensive negotiations and resources from public officials. The availability of these resources is based solely on political will and clout.

The political will available to Israel from foreign leaders has been limited even at the best of times. However, since 2009, it has diminished substantially. Over the past few years, Israel has placed itself on a collision course with European and US leaders over issues of human rights, settlements, and a lack of progress in the Israeli-Palestinian peace process. These issues have caused public opinion within these countries (as well as others) to deplete available political good will that might act as an impetus for collaborations with Israel. As a result, Israeli companies are finding that the barriers of doing business, especially in Europe and Asia, are slowly growing. In other places, relations have worsened to the point that Israeli companies that previously operated in these countries have closed shop.

Once a close ally, Turkey grew to become Israel's sixth largest trading partner, with civil trade reaching over 3.5

billion dollars a year. The ties between the two countries extended to academic research, mutual security interests, cultural and regional development projects and R&D collaboration efforts (through the respected offices of the Chief Scientists). In recent years, Israel has upgraded hundreds of Turkey's American-made tanks and military aircrafts. Turkey uses Israeli-produced drones against Kurdish guerrillas. And joint military exercises were conducted on a routine base. Yet Turkish-Israeli relations have suffered since Israel's 2008-2009 assault on Gaza, and reached a new low in May 2010 after Israel forcibly stopped a flotilla seeking to breach Israel's Gaza Strip sea blockade. The raid killed eight Turks and one Turkish-American citizen. Since the incident (and Israel's refusal to take responsibility for its outcome), the Turkish government has expelled the Israeli ambassador, suspended military links between the countries, and reduced funding for joint R&D activities. The overall climate has caused Israeli firms to shut down their operations in Turkey as they found that their client base in the country was disappearing. Israeli companies involved in military projects had to lay off their workers as well. One estimate calculated that Israel has lost between 8,000 and 10,000 jobs since 2010 as a direct result of the deterioration in Jerusalem- Ankara relations. This statistic does not account for additional damage to Israeli firms due to restrictions imposed on their operations. For example, Turkey has restricted the use of its airspace to Israeli cargo planes causing financial damage to Israeli aviation companies that must now use longer, less efficient routes to reach their destinations.

3. Access to talent

One by one the six Sumo wrestlers marched to center stage of the *dory* (土俵), a ring marked by rice-straw balls, constructed of clay and covered with sand. The six men split into two groups while stomping in a dance to please the spirits. One group approached the east corner as the other made its way toward the west. Once in position, the elder of one of the groups stepped forward, looked up, and tossed sacred salt to ask for peace from the Shinto gods.

In Japan, Sumo is more than a sport. According to religion, the very creation of the Japanese nation was the result of a Sumo match. The god Takemikazuchi won a Sumo bout and established the supremacy of the Japanese people on the island. At the *dory*, the match begins: two giants circle the ring, stop, turn to face one another, bow towards god, and then charge. Less than a minute passes and one of the giants is tossed outside the ring. The crowd cheers. Still, one can feel a certain lack of enthusiasm. Something is missing from this once great sport. Some say that the spirit has left, other people blame the young generation for turning its back on tradition. Regardless, the stadium is not full, nor is the excitement. Japanese people are coming less and less often to matches and the excitement and pride in the warriors on the part of those who do come are mixed with sorrow. This sorrow is due to the fact that the winner of this match was not Japanese but a hairy-chested Bulgarian named Kotooshu (Kalian Stefanov Mahlyanov).

The reason for this foreign invasion of a Japanese sport and its inevitable triumph is simple. The number of Japanese Sumo recruits dwindles each year. Sumo schools, or 'stables' as they are known, have been witnessing fewer and fewer new wrestlers entering through their gates as fewer young men are interested in this traditional path. This development paved the way for Kotooshu's unprecedented 2008 achievement of becoming the first European to win the Emperor's Cup. The shortage of interest from Japanese youth is placing the Japanese sport in danger of transforming and losing its native status.

The lack of talent in not unique to Japanese sport. Talent shortage is a global phenomenon, and it keeps top CEOs awake at night. Small businesses are finding it increasingly difficult to attract and retain people that will grow with their businesses and allow them to compete with larger firms. The attractive power of small companies is limited and constrained by their inability to compete with compensation packages offered by their more established rivals. Still, established firms that in the past have had access to promising candidates are finding that they too are faced with new challenges. Jim McNerney is one of the people whom this subject is keeping awake at night. Jim has managed large enterprises for over two decades. He has led companies such as GE and 3M through turbulent economic times and brought them to new heights. He is now the CEO of Boeing, the Seattle-based aerospace company that generated over 68 billion dollars in 2011 and employs over 160,000 people worldwide. Boeing has always struggled to find top engineers to build the world's leading aircrafts, but they may be now facing their biggest challenge yet. In the coming five years, over forty percent of Boeing's engineers will be eligible for retirement.

Since the 1980s, there has been a steady decline in the number of engineering graduates in the US. This has led to a growing gap between industry needs and the availability of educated, skilled workers. This gap is now widening exponentially with the retirement of the baby boomers. John Tracy, Boeing's Chief Technological Officer said of this shortage, "We have got to find ways to inspire students at all levels and from all backgrounds and cultures to become more interested in math and science and to pursue degrees in engineering."

The shortage of workers is not limited to the aerospace industry. Competition for talent, specifically in engineering, chemistry, advanced mathematics, and physics, as well as in top executive positions, is intensifying. This shortage of talent is a hard fact to accept, especially when looking at unemployment figures and college and university enrollment numbers, both of which are at an all-time high. Indeed, in 2009 the US alone produced some 38,000 graduates in computer and information science, more than 15,000 in mathematics and more than 11,000 in electrical engineering. These numbers would be impressive if it weren't for two caveats. The first is that in 1985, the US produced almost the exact number of graduates in these fields. In 1985 a little below 40,000 students graduated from computer science and 15,000 in mathematics. In 1985, the country graduated almost 20,000 students in electrical engineering, almost double the amount it graduated in 2009. However, the US did produce in 2009 more than double the amount of graduates it had produced in 1985 in visual and performing arts, psychology, and journalism.

The second caveat that affects the amount of available talent is the quality of education. Over the past thirty years, the standards of higher education for undergraduate degrees have decreased. As the financial burden associated with being a student has increased, the ability of Professors to demand more academic work from their students has decreased. As a result, a syllabus at a university class today is on average twenty-five percent shorter than it was in 1980. Demands on students are reduced in terms of reading, presentations, and integration of knowledge. The result of this deterioration is that the quality of new hires is not comparable to those thirty years ago. The effect of this situation is severe as it prevents companies from developing and growing. In a recent Manpower survey conducted on the availability of talent, forty-six percent of senior HR managers declared that "their talent gap was making it harder for their firm to implement its business strategy." Only twenty-seven percent said that they felt their businesses had the talent it needs. Furthermore, the report stated that while the global economic downturn may have masked this talent shortage for several years, the global recovery has made the strain of this talent shortage more evident. The shortage is not limited to the US or to developed countries, but is global in nature. Japan, India, and Brazil are also experiencing a severe shortage of talent. Employers there have stated that they "simply have an overall lack of applicants—they just aren't finding anyone available in their markets." (Talent Shortage Survey results 2011, Manpower)

*

The IMD World Competitive yearbook is an annually published report. The report's rankings measure how well countries manage their economic and human resources to increase their prosperity. Among its over three hundred and thirty ranking criteria is the availability of engineers. By this standard, Israel has been ranked in the top five for the past ten years running. Israel stays at this level mainly because of its ability to both grow and import skilled labor to fuel its economy. In addition, in the last IMD report, Israel ranked second only to Norway in the percentage of its population who has attained higher education. Israel's ongoing investments in education as a percentage of GDP are at the OECD average and have been relatively stable even through periods of low economic growth.

Such positive statistics are a surprise to many Israeli HR managers. A recent survey found that over one-third of all HR managers in Israel stated that they were failing, year after year, to meet recruiting targets for their companies. One HR manager told me that she was spending her evenings in bed reading CVs, searching between the lines for any indicator that a particular candidate might possess some of the skills and expertise needed by her development teams.

*

In the northern part of Tel-Aviv, the Barzel Street (literally 'road of iron') got its name from the garages and steel workshops that occupied the area in the 1970s. Today, the garages and workshops have moved to make way for glass office buildings that house some of Israel's most innovative high tech companies. Among these companies is SE, a leading data protection software firm, whose clients include Fortune 100 companies, banks, and government institutions.

The company is currently concerned with upgrading its software solution portfolio. The company's new products aim to reduce the management time associated with managing data security while not causing end users to feel restrained because of overprotective security concerns. One of SE's development team leaders is Shai. Shai is a programmer in his mid-thirties with short, curly hair that is beginning to gray, and a constant smile on his face. Over the past two years his team has grown from four developers to twenty. Still, the constant appearance of new clients with new demands and system-updating requirements make his team constantly understaffed. To meet his development goals, he has been recruiting at the pace of one new employee per month. Just before we met he was sending e-mails to his friends asking for help in identifying a database administrator (the person who is responsible for database performance and design) for his team. Because of the constant growth of his early stage company (SE was established less than five years ago) as well as the pressures and organization structure associated with all new companies, Shai needs a person who is relatively experienced. The experience he is after is not only in database management, but also in the security industry. This person must have specific skills and knowledge that are uncommon among standard database administrators.

Statistics about the availability of engineers in Israel is of little use to SE. The diversity of the industry has caused the title of engineer to be too inclusive. The high tech industry in which it operates has become so diverse that expertise has become extremely specific. Due to the division and subdivision of labor within the industry, each position has a set of associated sub-specifications of skills. As such, Shai is finding that there are very few applicants who possess the necessary experience that he seeks. Because his company is still in the early stage of its development, as most Israeli startups companies, and has a restricted amount of resources, he is not able to wait and invest the company's resources in proper training of the right person.

Unlike SE, Teva Pharmaceuticals has the size and breadth to develop the talent it requires. Teva is the worldwide leading generic pharmaceutical company. It was established over a century ago, has an annual income of over 18 billion dollars (2011), and employs over 40,000 people worldwide. About twenty years ago, Teva decided to place a significant emphasis on the creation of the chemicals that compose the active ingredients of its drugs (API). Although not a unique move in the industry, the capabilities that Teva developed in this area are second to none. One of Teva's leading manufacturing facilities that specializes in this production is located in Ramat Hovav, an industrial park in the southern part of Israel. The Ramat Hovav plant manufactures over one hundred different chemical products, most of which are so complex that

Teva is their sole producer. To preserve these capabilities, the company needs a constant supply of chemists and chemical engineers that have been trained for its specific needs. Due to the size and significance of the Ramat Hovav plant, the company has realized that, in the long term, it cannot afford to experience a shortage of qualified people nor compromise on the quality of its new recruits. This realization has caused the company to develop a proactive approach to recruitment. Teva offers scholarships to encourage people to study in specific fields, and they are working closely with the universities and colleges in the area to assure that their specific needs are included in the students' curricula. Furthermore, these academic institutions are also advising the company about potential candidates, to whom the company then offers internships for academic credit. This strategy is also beneficial for the academic institutions, as they are able to offer their students real industry experience and, to some at least, a job in one of the most advanced chemical facilities in the world. Nevertheless, this approach is valuable only for specific, entry-level positions. The challenge that many Israeli companies face lies not only attracting young and promising engineers, but also in attracting and creating experienced executives who are able to manage a global operation.

At the beginning of 2011, Shlomo Yanai, Teva's CEO since 2007, approached his board of directors and requested that he be allowed to step down from his post. During his term, Yanai had led the company through one of its most profitable eras. The company achieved an unprecedented eighteen concurrent quarters of growth that produced an annual average of seventeen percent growth. Through an aggressive merger & acquisition strategy and massive investments in internal developments, the company turned into a true multi-national firm with operations in over seventy production facilities around the world. Managing such a global firm requires skills and experience that Teva's board of directors would discover was not available in Israel. After almost a year of searching, the board decided to poach Jeremy Levin from Bristol-Myers Squibb, a US-based pharmaceutical company. Levin is an American executive with over twenty-five years of experience in the industry. He is an Oxford and

Cambridge graduate who has lived in six countries. By nominating Levin to be Teva's new CEO, the company's top two positions (CEO and Chairman) are now being held by non-Israelis for the first time.

*

When Israel achieved statehood in 1948, individuals living in British Mandate Palestine would receive everything from banking to health services from the ideological party they belonged to. These services also included education. When the state was founded, the political divide was so wide that the first government was reluctant to appoint a Minister of Education. In 1951, the Knesset (the Israeli parliament) started legislation for mandatory education. The legislative process shifted the debate to the concept of a unified education system. Over the next two years, protests aimed at maintaining the fragmented system were held throughout the country. Groups of young teenagers waving a red flag (associated with the workers' education system) and protesting against the notion of a unified education system, was a common scene on any given Friday afternoon.

In 1953, after a long struggle, David Ben-Gurion, Israel's first Prime Minister was able to unite some of the systems under the government. However, because of political pressure he was forced to create two competing systems: the General system and the General Religious system. The new legislation placed both systems under the supervision of the new Ministry of Education. Two other systems remained outside the scope of the law. These systems were allowed to continue to operate under some restrictions, but with no or little supervision. The systems included the Independent Ultra-Orthodox system and the Arab system. The rationale for this division was that Ben-Gurion believed that the first group would not continue to exist much. The common belief at the time was that religious groups would integrate into the general population within a generation. Ben-Gurion did not want to alienate the ultra-orthodox thereby preventing an integration process he believed was already taking place. In the Arab education system, government policies were similar to the general one, with some adjustments. The system would have the same obligations and the same curriculum as the Jewish system, but with adjustments, such as studying Hebrew as a second language and being more open to local Arab leaders requests.

Ben-Gurion's hope that the independent ultra-orthodox system would slowly fade away did not materialize. Sixty years later, the independent ultra-orthodox system not only did not disappear, it mushroomed. The system has grown to monstrous proportions, passing tens of thousands of children through its gates under no meaningful government supervision. The Israeli Ministry of Education has little to say about the quality of its facilities and the basic infrastructure of its schools. The Ministry has even less control over the system's curriculum and the quality of its teachers.

The children within independent ultra-orthodox schools focus primarily on religious studies, and graduates of these schools find that they lack knowledge and skills associated with math, science, English language, and other subjects that would allow them to better integrate into the general society. The scope and severity of the problems associated with this system are best seen in people who have chosen to leave the ultra-orthodox lifestyle. In 2004, the Knesset conducted a hearing within the Parliament's Education Committee on the matter. During the hearing, a twenty-seven year-old man by the name of Israel Rotur testified before the committee. "We used to go to school at seven and return home late at night," he said. "We studied stories of richest man and discussed biblical verses ... but I never studied English or math, I didn't even know what the Knesset is, the building I am in today, as we were never thought civics.... At the age of twenty I had to start studying everything from scratch while trying to support myself. Today I am twenty-seven and after a long battle I was able to put myself in a position where I have a chance of obtaining an under-graduate degree."

Some alumni of the system who have detached themselves from the ultra-orthodox community joined together to sue the government for negligence (2000). These plaintiffs claimed that the government's actions (or lack thereof) prevented them from pursuing competitive professions and integrate into Israel's general society. In this case the Supreme Court ruled that the obligation of the government to provide education is limited to the obligations of 'accessibility,' meaning only that every child should go to school, and 'adaptability,' meaning that the school could be adapted to the way of life of the student and not necessarily to that of the general population.

The problems with the Arab system are less severe than those of the ultra-orthodox system. Government expenditure on education per student within the Arab system is at similar levels to those in the general system, but a gap of quality continues to exist. Later in life, this gap widens. The quality gap is caused by differing quality of teachers and curriculum. Although students in each system are supposed to study the same subjects, the fact that Hebrew is taught as a second language in the Arab system, in a country where the economic life is conducted in Hebrew, causes later inequality in terms of access to higher education and employment. In addition to the curriculum and quality of the schools, the economic conditions of the two populations also influence the ability of their students to pursue higher education. Taken together, these factors create a growing gap between students' levels of education. As such, it is more likely to find Arab students studying Hebrew literature in university than engineering simply because the entry barrier for the latter is so much higher.

In 1960, these two systems, the Arab and the Independent Ultra-Orthodox system, serviced only fifteen percent of all Israeli school children. Today, they serve more than half of Israeli school children. The quality gap between the systems and the number of students within them is a cause of great concern for future economic integration. An OECD study estimated that Israel could gain an increase of fifteen percent of its GDP just by making equal the systems at the secondary school level (ages 12–18). This estimate does not account for the possibility of higher participation in higher education, which would lead to almost a double contribution in GDP per capita.

As the economy grows, it requires more workers. Since the Israeli economy has grown in the direction of a knowledge-based economy, workers will need to possess skills that are currently not being fostered within half of the country's population. In the past, Israel was able to obtain its workforce by encouraging immigration from the Soviet Union. The current Israeli economy owes a lot to the over one million immigrants who arrived briefly after the collapse of the Soviet Union. Over twenty percent of the immigrants who arrived during that period and who were a part in the workforce (ages 15-67) had engineering backgrounds. Within less than five years, the average income of these new immigrants was ninety-five percent of that of the average population. This indicates that they where able to fully integrate into the workforce in a relatively short period of time. This boost of highly educated people was able to kick start a period of massive growth in Israel. A recent article in *The Economist* captures the challenges that face Israel as it moves forward: "The Soviet Union is not going to collapse again, Israel is not going to get another million Russians."

*

After 1983, Ireland went through a series of reforms that were intended to promote economic growth. In 1994, it emphasized reforms that would promote education and training. From 1993 to 2000, the Irish government nearly doubled its expenditure per student. In addition to this effort, it established training grants that covered the full payroll cost of trainings for employees. This allowed companies to lower the costs of their training programs and hence truly invest in the development of their workforces. To preserve the country's competitiveness, the government went though reforms designed to manage wage inflation. The government accomplished this through grants that were directed at employers and were accompanied by macro-economic measures that were aimed at reducing consumer index levels. In addition, immigration reforms, taken years earlier, allowed for a continuous flow of workers when local supply was insufficient. This series of programs and legislation led the Irish economy into one of its most prosperous periods. Continuing these policies, even in the midst of the financial crisis that hit the country's financial sector and caused the country to nearly go insolvent, allowed the Irish economy to bounce back relatively quickly in comparison to other European countries.

Ireland's government reforms were designed to support domestic companies' ability to access talent in two forms—internally through education and continuous trainings and externally through immigration. These two pillars of policy were accompanied by an understanding that access to talent needs to be conducted in a way that will serve companies' overall competitiveness. That is to say, these companies should be able to find the people they need at prices that will not constrain their ability to offer their services at competitive prices.

The Ireland case shows that the talent problem can be addressed by paying attention to four topics: education, training, immigration, and macroeconomic activity that support's industry competitiveness in terms of compensation.

*

Over the past few years, Israeli students' performance on standard math and science tests has declined relative to that of students in other countries. This is not to say that the level of public education has declined, but rather that the world is pressing forward and Israel is not catching up. The questions policymakers often ask are: Where do I look? What are best practices? How can I implement these practices? The most common answers to these questions is Finland.

Some may argue that Finish innovation peaked with the creation of 'wife carrying' (an actual sport where male competitors race while carrying a female teammate), but Finland also brought us the video game Angry Birds. Juvenile as these two examples may seem, they display the elements of complexity and simplicity that have secured Finland the top rank on the INSIAD innovation-ranking index. This ranking is a direct result of the very best education system in the world. Every year education professionals from around the world visit Finland to try to learn the best educational practices. Few, however, are able to implement the qualities of the Finnish system, as it is based on culture, tradition, and needs that do not necessarily apply to other countries.

Instead of going to Finland and trying to revolutionize our system, we should start with something much more basic—our teachers. It's easy to say that we need better teachers. Some even suggest that we fire them all and hire only perfect teachers, teachers that would provide our children with the very best, teachers that will be so smart that knowledge will fills the very air they breathe, teachers that are so talented that after only an hour their students will be able to apply advanced problem solving methods. The problem with these teachers is that they do not exist. Even the best teachers—those who possess just a fraction of such skills—are faced with a working environment that is not supportive, motivating or rewarding. Policymakers can start by making the teachers' job environment one that rewards excellence, provides the flexibility to adapt to specific needs, and allows them to try new things and innovate. We also need to focus on evaluating our teachers, not with the aim of punishing below average achievers, but to provide real and meaningful feedback about their performance. We can help teachers become better by training them or simply by helping them focus on their strengths and improve their weaknesses. Only by helping teachers become better and more motivated will we be able to help students get the most out of their teachers.

Education does not stop at school or the university graduation ceremony, it continues through various types of trainings. Managers often say that people are their most important asset. Still, these managers often fall short when they need to invest in training their employees. In Israel, only a small number of companies invest in training. Sometimes this is due to lack of awareness, but more often it's due to financial constraints. The Israeli economy is based mostly on micro-companies with fewer than twenty employees, and these types of companies cannot afford to invest in training programs. By providing financial incentives, policymakers can encourage firms to further train their employees so they can continue to learn, to develop new skills, to keep up with industry advances, and to become ever more competitive—long after they have left the formal education systems.

Unlike education, discussion of immigration policies is a statistically-proven method of sending politicians straight into a political graveyard. The truth of the matter is that immigration policies have had, both in the past and present, tremendous impact on the economic development of all countries. In current debates, governments often like to create a distinction between low-skilled and high-skilled immigration. However, both forms are needed to advance economic activity. Low-skilled labor is a major part of any economy, even those based on high technology sectors. These immigrants allow for price reductions in labor-intensive activities allowing companies to be competitive through all stages of their respected value chain. Highly skilled immigrants are able to provide skills, which may not be developed or widely available in a country. When constructing immigration policies, the line between the two is hard to define. It is also complicated to declare the extent to which one group can enter a country and another cannot. Regardless of where this line passes, governments can help their companies by lowering the administrative burdens associated with obtaining work permits and other legal authorizations.

It is true that every immigration policy has social implications. Nevertheless, confronting these implications by means of an all-or-nothing approach in which no immigration is allowed and the companies who do wish to use immigrant labor are faced with administrative burdens aimed solely at disincentivizing the companies seeking these workers has serious economic implications. Such burdens result in immigrant workers being available only to large successful companies that possess the administrative capabilities to import workers, while small companies are left in the dust.

4. Access to Infrastructure

Frederick Barbarossa the first was a German king of the 12th century. In addition to being king, he carried the title of Holy Roman Emperor. He was a true European leader, with dominions from Germany through Italy, France, and Spain. Among his greatest accomplishments was the unification of the German empire, the restoration of peace in Bavaria, and perhaps most importantly, the construction of the port of Hamburg in the year 1189. The port of Hamburg allowed the city to establish itself as the 'Gateway of Europe'. In past centauries, the people of Hamburg were known for being among the richest in the world, thanks to the trade and business that the port provided. It was there that the America Line Company was created, connecting first Europe to North America and then running lines all over the world. By 1850, the company was the largest shipping company in the world; three times the size of the British East-India Company.

A millennium later, the Hamburg port is still one of the largest ports in the world. The port is responsible for the employment of over 100,000 people (about ten thousand are directly employed by the port). In 2011, it handled over 130 million tons of cargo that had been generated from over 10,000 ships. Even during the recent recession, the port increased the amount of cargo it handled by nine percent. Nevertheless, it's ability to continue increase its cargo handling capacity is questionable. Last year, the port experienced what it called 'significant congestion,' as did the two other large European ports, Rotterdam and Antwerp. This delayed cargo transport and left ships waiting in the open sea for days, until the port could allow them to enter.

Capacity constraints are not limited to sea traffic. Logistic pressures are felt around the world on all types of transport infrastructure: roads, rail and air. There are few people on the planet today who do not feel the effects of congested infrastructure. Air traffic has become routinely jammed, making flight delays and cancellations routine. In European countries, construction of new roads and highways are behind that of traffic growth by a factor of almost two, making daily commutes longer.

When done right, infrastructure investments have the potential to transform entire economies. Examples of this action are plenty in countries like Singapore, Ireland, New Zealand, and Norway. Despite its disadvantage of being remote, New Zealand has become an export-based economy with major trade partners in Asia, Europe and North America. Ireland used infrastructure investments as the backbone of its transformation to an information-based economy, offering services on a global scale, from advanced R&D to low-key tech support. These investments not only allow businesses to be more efficient and more competitive, they also create innovation.

Infrastructure projects, by nature, are huge. They represent the largest financial investments in the world. They are also technologically driven. Walking through the warehouses of the Hamburg port, one cannot overlook the technological advances this port has included in its structure. These massive capital investments also entail a constant search for improvements in productivity. These improvements have a huge impact on the return on capital ratio across multiple areas. Given this fact, innovation that can materialize productivity potential in infrastructure projects, is an area that attracts a lot of investment.

*

Skolkovo University has an unusual, futuristic architectural design. The campus is structured as a disk with four differently sized buildings located on its roof and expanding toward the exterior. Walking through the green plains surrounding the structure one will notice that the buildings themselves are built to resemble a kind of prism through which the surrounding landscape can be viewed in a light that changes as the day progresses. The university, founded in 2006, is just a few kilometers West of Moscow. Among its main occupants is a business school that was designed and built by the Russian business community. From its earliest stages, the academic faculty formed partnerships with leading institutions such as MIT, the Russian Economic School and Stanford to bring the school the best lecturers and research. After only four years of operation, the school launched a new initiative to transform the school and its surroundings into a Russian-made Silicon Valley. This new 'valley' is driven by the local business community and the Russian government, who have committed over 4 billion dollars for the first phase of the project. Most of this investment is allocated into spaces that will allow entrepreneurs to study, work, and live. In the same time, the government is working to attract major companies that will act as 'anchor businesses' from which new businesses can learn, support, and emerge. Among the companies who have set up joint projects and facilities to support this aim are Intel, IBM, and BP.

The Russian example of building a university campus that can attract business and create innovation is not unfamiliar. Many countries have implemented this concept in different parts of the world. However, this notion of "if you build it, they will come" (Kevin Costner, *Field of Dreams*) has failed more often than not. The government of Malaysia, for example, decided that, like many governments around the world, its economic future lay in biotechnology. The government created and heavily invested in a 'Bio Valley' campus, which was intended to bring together the top minds of the country and abroad in order to conduct biotechnology-based research, that would later mature into successful businesses. The government tried to attract local players by advertising and provided financial incentives designed to attract foreign firms. The core of the project was a two thousand acre site with three research institutions and state-of-the-art equipment. Five years later, the site has won the nickname 'bio-ghost valley'. This example is only one of many from both developed and developing countries. Studies in the field of government intervention for supporting entrepreneurship in the form of creating new facilities show similar results. Publicly funded science parks have been shown to create less growth in employment or venture capital investments than parks developed without government support.

*

Alon Hasson is a large man. He weighs well over 150 kilograms. His hair, which is cut short, is beginning to gray, and he has a baby face and a pleasant quiet manner that quickly wins you over. However, don't let his baby face mislead you, Alon is considered one of the strongest men in Israel. In his position he controls the largest port in Israel, which is able to handle over one million containers annually. Alon is not the manager of the port, but rather the leader of the workers' union. From his early childhood, Alon knew that he did not want to work in a place like the port. But his father, a Moroccan Jew who immigrated to Israel in the early 1960s, pushed him to find a steady job for a good company. So when Alon turned twenty-one, he found a job with his dad disembarking ships. In 1998, at the age of twenty-eight, he was elected a member of the port's union organization board. Five years later, he was elected the chairman of the union.

His office is filled with pictures of rabbis and festive events in Morocco, which connect him to his family's heritage. In his office he tends to walk in circles, talking on one of his two cell phones as the sound of the office other landline phones never stops. In 2011, Alon led the port of Ashdod in over thirty days of strikes and sanctions (including an 'Italian strike', in which all the port's workers called in sick). His actions caused an estimated 1.5 billion dollars in losses for Israeli business. That year, disruption in the port's operations became routine to the point that the CEO of IKEA came to the port personally for a meeting with Alon, begging that his cargo be released. The conflict started first as a coordinated strike with participation of all Israeli seaports and was backed by the national labor union (Histadrout). However, the Ashdod strikes continued long after the coordination ended. Any time that Alon felt that an employee's rights were not respected or were at risk, the port would shut down. In one case, the management asked to change an incentive program in which, on a monthly basis, the team that would disembark the largest number of ships would receive a meal at a local restaurant (valued at less than 100 dollars!). This change led to a more than fifty percent drop in production speed. In another case, delays were caused by the birthday party of Alon's twelve-year-old daughter, as employees asked to come and congratulate the chairman.

It is not just seaports that cause disruption. The Israeli railway is also known for its constant delays (As I write this paragraph, the Israeli Rail is on strike). In 2011, the Ben-Gurion airport was shut down twice because of labor disputes. The disruption in sea and airports, as well as rail traffic not only causes direct damage to importers and exporters, but also creates additional costs, as businesses invest in ways to cope with uncertainty and reliability issues of basic infrastructure and adapt business models accordingly. These business models refrain from using public transport, prefer costly air transport over sea, invest in insurance and guarantees in case of any halt in transport infrastructure, avoid production in Israel altogether, or limit the growth of their businesses voluntarily.

*

In 2005, the Israeli government adopted a plan to develop the southern part of Israel, the Negev. The plan called for the creation of clusters of technology development areas within the proximity of the Ben-Gurion University in the Negev. As part of this plan, Israeli military hi-tech units were instructed to relocate to the area. Plans for facilities that would accommodate research institutions and large international companies, were approved and construction was scheduled. The plan was later presented to US-based investors and officials who nicknamed the project "a Bulgarian approach to regional development."

The top-down approach, in which government creates

all the facilities, attract entrepreneurs into a center, and help gather funding, has been tried in Israel countless times and failed just as often, like in most cases around the world.

The leaders of the city of the Tel-Aviv municipally decided to take a different approach. In a recent interview with *The Wall Street Journal*, Ron Huldai, the mayor of Tel-Aviv, said: "Tel Aviv (in past) had become a city that people used, not a city they lived in. We are creating a good place for hi-tech people to live in, I am doing it for the people working in hi-tech." This statement reflects a bottom-up approach for supporting business. Instead of dictating the path for development, the city allowed the local community to develop itself as it saw fit.

Indeed, the community developed in ways that the government could not have foreseen. Instead of government-built boardrooms and offices, in Tel-Aviv it is common to see people with laptops working from one of the city's over 800 cafés and restaurants, most of which offer free Wi-Fi. As apposed to the Skolkovo center's recreation spaces, people in Tel-Aviv finish their workday by going to one of the city's 500 pubs to unwind and network. Tel-Aviv's infrastructure provides one café per 500 inhabitants and one pub per 800 inhabitants. No government in the world would be able to justify such an investment.

Gideon and Nimrod are the two founders of IQWind, a truly innovative company that has won numerous awards for the development of a variable gear technology (IQgear). This technology significantly reduces the cost of energy generated by both existing and newly built wind turbines.

In the US, there are stories of companies who started in garages; IQWind started in restaurants and cafés. When the company wanted to hold large team meetings or needed space for other purposes, they would sit together at 'New-York New-York', a hamburger restaurant, just north of Tel-Aviv, with a large almost deserted second floor. When they needed space for more individual work, they would gather in a café near Macabi Park on the eastern side of Tel-Aviv. This approach allowed them to not worry about financing office space and communications at the early stages of their enterprise. Instead, the company's two founders focused on building computer-generated models and commissioning lab work. Only once this part had been completed and the team grew and its needs began to accrue in a more structured manner, did they seek proper accommodation.

The Tel-Aviv approach to development might be called "worry about the people and the people will do the rest." In a country where garages are uncommon, the people of Tel-Aviv found alternative environments in which to establish their businesses. These environments took the form of cafés and bars. For Tel-Aviv this approach proved an effective one. The city now houses more than six hundred companies in the early stages of development. These companies attract more venture capital than any other region, and they create pressure on communication providers to install the fastest Internet connections available.

5. Access to predictable, sensible and reliable regulation

I was in Rome, participating in a lunch organized by the European Union Chambers of Commerce in China under the name 'Perspectives on Italian Business in China'. The event provided a unique opportunity to engage with both Chinese executives and Europeans who conduct regular business in China. At the break from the presentations, I was wandering the lobby joining different groups discussions. A common theme in these discussions and one that surprised me was the participants' confidence in the Chinese government. This confidence was delivered in a manner that is in distinct contrast to the sentiments held by the citizens of the US, Europe and Israel towards their own governments. Dozens of business leaders shared the belief that China's leaders possessed the foresight to see the challenges ahead as well as the courage to act and meet those challenges. Both the Chinese and European delegates recognized the existence of bubbles in parts of the Chinese economy; they recognized that, although preserving their export position, the undervaluation of the Renminbi had taken a toll on the economy. They all understood that the Chinese economy needed to increase consumption and imports and that this would come at a cost for some of the businesses operating in China and may be accompanied by social unrest. These challenges were clear to all of the participants, and they were open and willing to talk about these challenges. Yet, they saw these challenges with the belief that these problems are surmountable, that they can be overcome.

Mostly, these delegates displayed a faith in the government's commitment and ability to take action and implement policies that would keep the Chinese economy in good health. I asked how one obtains such faith, and was given three reasons as an answer. The first is pure propaganda. The limitation of choice and criticism that people who live in free democracies find repulsive is the same thing that provides these officials with their faith. The next two factors, however, are factors that we should envy and try hard to implement within our own systems.

Predictability - The Chinese government is by all

accounts predictable. We know that the Renminbi is manipulated, but we also know that it is going to remain so for the next five years, and that it's going to depreciate at a determined rate during these five years. We know this simply because the Chinese government declared that this process is part of a five-year plan. This is simply their way of implementing the plan. The source of this predictability is a general stability. Changes in government are minor. Within the government there is no one who rises from obscurity into power. Everyone, from a high-level cabinet minister to a mid-level bureaucrat, has held and moved through the chains of power in a long process, during which he has proven himself in one form or another. This process allows one to understand how an official behaved in the past, how he forms his opinions and executes his powers, and thus how he will proceed in the future.

Responsibility - In addition to being predictable, the Chinese government is responsible. Free from the need to secure popular approval, Chinese officials can implement constant, yet modest, changes as they are needed. This also provides the government with the ability to implement long-term strategies, as they are free from the need to constantly display short-term successes. Despite the positive dimensions of these powers, we should remember that this ability to form policies that are detached from public opinion includes less pleasant consequences. One major consequence is the over-involvement of the government in the Chinese economy and in the day-to-day operations of business within their territory.

In contrast, Western systems have historically worked to ease businesses' dependence on government and to allow them to act independently of government. Still, such measures have more to do with the daily operations of businesses and not their long-term survival. Government still has a major role to play in setting the overall environment in which businesses operate. In the West, this overall system, despite being filled with ideals of freedom, transparency and equality, is shadowed by specters of populism and ever-changing regulatory themes. The inability of businesses to predict their governments' policies and actions generates a sense of instability. As Howard Schultz, the CEO of Starbucks, said on CNN's Piers Morgan show about the role of government "The government needs to produce a foundation of confidence.... People and businesses need to have faith and confidence in what the leaders are doing, why they are doing it, and there has to be a collective understanding about what's in it for them." An absence of a sense of confidence can cause businesses to become reluctant to make major investment decisions. This reluctance to invest can be seen today in the largest companies in the US. These companies would rather hold onto their capital than invest it or deliver it to their shareholders. At the end of 2011, Apple had over 30 billion dollars in cash and short-term investments, Microsoft had 51 billion dollars, Pfizer had 26 billion dollars, Coca-Cola had 14 billion dollars and the list of unused capital goes on.

To further understand this uncertainty one should look at a recent example, the US Patient Protection and Affordable Care Act (also known as US healthcare reform or Obamacare). The bill requires businesses operating in the US to invest in and change their healthcare-related obligations towards their employees. These changes carry some costs to business. Currently, the Republican Party promises to repeal the bill. Although this notion is improbable, it has caused business to wait on its investments. This is because they are in an environment in which major legislation and its impact on business is not clear. It's not only major regulations that have a fog of uncertainty around them. Industry-specific regulation is sometimes even harder to predict. A McKinsey analysis about the value at stake from such regulation found that, globally, companies might lose up to 800 billion dollars in operation income from such industry-specific regulation. The report continued by saying that "the huge regulatory impact of the crisis in just a few sectors doesn't mean that executives in other ones can relax. Telcos, transport and logistics companies, energy providers, retailers, pharma companies, and health care providers have long been subject to extensive government intervention."

Faced with the need to maintain and speak to popular opinion, regulators sometimes feel the need to become extremely direct and specific about the corporate or social behavior they expect. In these cases, instead of providing a proper regulatory environment, legislators find themselves in a position where they try to dictate how each player should act.

The 2010 Dodd-Frank Act set an ambitious goal. It aimed to prevent a financial crisis like the one that the world has recently experienced. Its strategy was sensible: improve transparency, stop banks from taking excessive risk and prevent abusive financial practices. However, the way in which the act was written was complex and painfully specific. In an attempt to prevent specific actions they perceived as neglect, its authors attempted to predict every contingency which, financial institutions might try to take. The authors tried to predict every eventuality and to dictate what is right and what is wrong for banks to do in every foreseeable situation. The notion that legislators should focus on specific actions within the business environment and govern every eventuality is not new. In the US, legislators have prevented the selling of peanuts in Lee County, Florida, after sundown on Wednesdays. They have also stated that in counties in Alabama with populations between 56,500 and 59,000 people, domino games shall be lawful in billiard rooms or any other rooms in which billiard tables are located.

When legislators implement regulations that lack clarity and simplicity, they provoke voices that preach for the abolishment of all regulation. However, market economies cannot function properly without rules that protect private property and ensure fair competition. Regulation is also a means of preserving a country's broader interests. Such interests include consumer protection, safety and environmental protections. The ability to balance these interests with the imperatives of economic development is a tricky one, and it usually requires a degree of trial and error, as well as the ability to be dynamic, yet predictable. It is very easy to get it wrong. Getting it right, however, can unleash creativity in magnitudes that can change millions of lives for the better. Western democracies have an advantage in unleashing this potential. If the Chinese have a five-year plan, Western countries have ideals and dreams. It may not sound like much, but creativity usually favors dreams over plans. Yet, sustainable growth requires a mixture of both.

*

In May 2010, members of the OECD accepted Israel as the organization's thirty-third member country. In its first economic survey of the country officials from the organization wrote that "in many respects Israel's short, but dramatic history has created a combination of economic, social, demographic and political circumstances without close parallel to any other OECD member country." Even the country's most outspoken critics cannot argue that Israel is less than an incredible economic success story. Confronted with challenges that would have crippled a country ten times its size, Israel has emerged as one of the world's leading economies, with innovative thinkers and doers, Nobel Prize laureates and many renowned business leaders. In the midst of crises and faced with real and immediate challenges, Israel was able to construct effective regulatory policies (e.g., Yozma, the country's banking policies after the 1980s crash, monetary policies after hyperinflation and healthcare reforms in the early 1990s). These policies, however, have been mostly formed as responses to crises. To assume a leading role in the international sphere, Israel must take its tradition of implementing robust and effective regulation and extend it to times of peace and calm. To understand the areas where such regulation needs to be focused, it should rely on reviews by the OECD, the

World Bank and economic think tanks to identify common themes across these publications. These themes can help policymakers to focus on implementing or changing current regulations. In this respect, Israel is in luck. There are only two such regulatory themes that are constantly repeated in every economic review that is done on the country. If addressed by regulators, these themes can prove to have a significant impact on the country's economy. They are *transparency* and *enforcement*.

Transparency

The Japanese government has been for many years one of the Palestinian Authority's main contributors. After many years of continuous contributions that were aimed at building a future Palestinian state (around 150 million dollars a year since 1993), the Japanese Special Envoy to the Middle East requested a detailed account from the Authority about the uses of these contributions. After two months, the Special Envoy received a letter from Yasser Arafat, the former Chairman of the Palestinian Authority and leader of the PLO. In this letter, Arafat began detailing the struggles and challenges that the Palestinian people face, then he went on to emphasize their need for support and his appreciation of the Japanese people's friendship and commitment in building a Palestinian state. After this elaborate introduction, Arafat finished his letter by saying "I would like to assure you with this letter that the funds provided by the Japanese government were properly spent."

Transparency is more than just non-corrupt governance; it is a way for people and businesses to understand the direction that their countries are taking. It is the ability to understand the resources that may be available, as well as those that may fall short, and by that, to plan and form strategies. The main document that contains a government's policies and their effects on business is the government's budget. The best practice for such documents is to describe, in details, all of the country's resources and allocations. Best practice documents also include a detailed account of the previous year's allocations and the impact these resources have had on different areas of operations and policy.

Not all such documents around the world provide the same details, nor are they all constructed in the same way. The US budget book is considered to be one of the longest and most detailed. On average, it is twice as long as Tolstoy's *War and Peace*, not including the full list of allocations. Under Tony Blair, the UK took a step toward further transparency by beginning to include well-defined targets that government actions should achieve. This included, for example, the time it takes the police to arrive to a crime scene or high school dropout rate. Unlike the US full budget that requires a cart to carry, the Israeli budget is only around one hundred and twenty pages long. Its chapters are divided by ministries, with the top line indicating the individual ministry's total budget for the year. The rest of the chapter is filled with tables and terms that are understandable to no one. At the end of the chapter, there are remarks that explain the rationale of allocation. Looking at the budgets of years passed, one finds that the majority of these remarks have stayed the same, word for word, regardless of the financial situation or the identity of the ruling government. This practice does allow the government a measure of flexibility as it can reallocate resources, although with some constraints, throughout the year. Yet the practice also means that the different ministries have difficulty spending their budgets because they require constant approval from the Ministry of Finance. As such, the practice leads to ministries not being able to spend their approved budgets. Some ministries are able to spend less than seventy percent of their approved budgets. The practice of obscurity, with the budget as the leading document that serves as a model for government, reaches down into other areas of government. To put this in business terms, the government is not clearly signaling the country's direction and future actions. By not doing so, businesses working within the scope of government (either by providing services or simply being affected by the government actions) are operating in a world that is filled with unnecessary uncertainties.

Enforcement

The World Bank's business report indicates that Israel is a relatively satisfactory place to start a business. It is ranked fifth in terms of 'protecting investors,' and it is ranked tenth in 'ease of trading across borders.' Nevertheless, Israel ranks 43rd (2012) in the aggregated ranking because of an inability to enforce contracts (for which it is ranked 94th as of 2012). It takes an average of 515 days to receive a trial and afterwards judgment, and it takes another 360 days to be able to enforce the court's ruling. The inability to enforce contracts and regulation is a main cause of uncertainty and risk in placing investments in Israel. The fact that enforcing contracts is difficult leads businesses to raise barriers for doing business with Israeli firms (e.g., placing bonds or capital as assurance), which further limits companies' ability to operate.

*

There is no guideline to good regulation however, common themes do emerge from the literature concerning regulation, most of which are:

- *Experience-based regulation:* countries are not isolated entities. They operate in an international environment that holds vast experience and wisdom. More often than not, any given challenge has already been faced by another country (e.g.

Yozma mentioned earlier is based on a successful US initiative). It is true that there is no one-size-fits-all solution. However, proper analysis of actions and the effects of past regulation can prevent the reoccurrence of pitfalls that have already been experienced elsewhere.

- *Fact-based regulation:* Regulators are populists by nature. They tend to take cases that have been covered in the media and are familiar to the public. This allows them to articulate their message. The media, however, often portrays the extraordinary, not the ordinary, nor the factual. Facts, especially economic facts, are boring; they are published in mathematical figures and tables, which are appealing to few. Despite their boring nature, these are the facts that need to be studied, analyzed and modeled in order to create good regulation.
- *Dynamic regulation:* Regulation should be a trial-and-error process, rather than a singular event. This notion is a hard sell, as regulators are faced with constant political pressures. Dynamic regulation requires them to face these pressures

on a continuous basis. Regulators can, however, adopt 'sunset' clauses that force regulation to be regularly reviewed and amended.

- *Evenly enforced regulation:* Competition requires that everyone play by the same rules. Regulators should be neutral in their approach to the players. They should level the playing field by lowering entry barriers to newcomers and assure there is no discrimination embedded in the market place toward one or another type of company.
- *Simple regulation:* It is human nature to complicate things. Companies tend to create layers of complexity as a means to higher barriers of entrance. At the basic level, however, all companies operate in the same way: they buy basic goods, adjust them, combine them in some way, and sell them back to consumers. By unveiling layers of complexity and composing simple and coherent regulation, legislators can avoid the mistake of being too particular and create unfair loopholes.

6. Culture and social networks

At the end of 2011, I moved from a relatively successful career in management consulting into an operational role within a pharmaceutical company. After a few months in my new role, I gave a presentation for which I received excellent reviews, from both fellow managers and the CEO of the company. Reflecting on my performance and the document that I had presented, I came to realize that the thinking I put forward, the overall trends I had described and my analysis of these trends were the result of numerous conversations that I had conducted during the preceding weeks, most with people outside my own company. The people who provided me with the most information and those who most powerfully challenged my own assumptions were members of a larger network of which I was a part. This network of people shared my interests and knowledge. It was created spontaneously, yet it flourished to the point that I could derive from it real value.

The notion of networks and their contribution in our day-to-day life has been studied and written about extensively, however this was the first time I had noticed its impact on my own work. Basically, an informal network is a platform for transporting large amounts of knowledge and information. Networks increase the value of collaboration as they reduce the price of searching for information, validating that information, and engaging with people in meaningful ways.

Within any given company, one can count dozens, if not hundreds, of these networks and they often expand beyond the company's boundaries. These networks are usually formed across a common theme. There are networks based on profession (e.g., networks of strategy or operation), some of which are based around a particular industry with participants from different and competing companies. Other networks include alumni groups from a particular university or a past company; still others are based on geographical origin, religion, and ethnicity. Among these different types of networks, the ones that people find most reliable, easy to use, and easy to get involved in, are those networks based on ethnicity. These are also the networks that are the largest and easiest to identify.

There are more than twenty million Indian people living abroad; there are three times as many Chinese people living outside Mainland China. These people are disproportionately better educated and more highly skilled than their European and Anglo-Saxon counterparts. They are also well positioned in the business world, as they serve various functions across many large multinational corporations. Research conducted by UC Berkeley Dean & social network expert, Annalee Saxenien found that over half of all Indians working in Silicon Valley had advised entrepreneurs within India, and that eighteen percent actively invested in Indian companies. A second study, conducted by Taro Khanna, a professor at the Harvard Business School, found that firms that have contacts with members of the Indian diaspora have performed better than others in the same region. No other social networks offer the same reach nor value as those that are based on ethnicity.

Knowledge of the value of social networks is not new, nor is it exclusive to business. The Israeli secret service agency, the Mossad, is known for using Jewish networks across the world in order to obtain information and, in cases of emergency, transport goods and people. This allows the intelligence organization to be one of the smallest in the world, yet at the same time the most effective and renowned.

Just like the Mossad, Israeli companies use unofficial networks constantly. They do so in two ways. The first involves tapping into the current knowledge of the network's participants. This enables companies to understand and obtain the most up-to-date information about the industry, as well as analysis of recent moves different players strategies. The second way that Israeli companies use their networks is to establish trust and to collaborate.

To an outsider, the world may appear filled with borders and boundaries. Even in the developing world, collaborating is a challenge. Different regulations, procedures, languages, and customs make it hard to establish business relations that involve the transfer of money and goods. Even when dealing in countries where the rule of law is certain, the cost of potential litigation in these foreign places may reduce the probability of cooperation. It is human nature to deal with those we trust and in which we have confidence. Personal ties make risks easier to mitigate.

Elad is a Gilat alumnus. After he left Gilat, Elad formed a venture aimed at connecting villages in sub-Saharan Africa through use of a two-way satellite communication device. His company developed a cheap means of manufacturing and maintaining this equipment and his business model offers African small businesses the opportunity to lease the equipment and pay per use. It is difficult for any small company to conduct business in Africa, especially in rural areas of the continent, which are the places Elad's company is most interested in. Despite these hurdles, Elad is managing quite well, mainly thanks to a middleman, an Israeli named Eyal, who lives in Nigeria. Eyal runs an export business, and Elad trusts his middleman, partly because the two are ethnic kin, and partly because an Israeli middleman needs to maintain a good reputation. If a middleman cheats one Israeli, all the others with whom he does business will soon know about it. News travels fast within informal networks.

*

As the Indian diaspora creates incredible value to the Indian economy, so should the Israeli government understand and cherish its own diaspora. It should make an effort to ensure that the diaspora cares for its origin, and it should collaborate with the diaspora while helping its individuals achieve their own goals, regardless of their location. Currently, the attitude toward the diaspora is less one of willing collaboration and more of a notion of lost children that need to be guided home. A recent campaign by the Israeli government expressed this clearly; a television & online campaign directed at Israeli expats, urged them to come back to Israel. One of the ads featured a young boy who attempted to get his father's attention with the word 'daddy'; he finds more success when he uses the word 'abba,' which is Hebrew for father. The slogan for the campaign was: "They will always remain Israelis. Their children may not." This campaign caused consternation and disgust in expats and Jewish communities around the world, with the Jewish Federations of North America (JFNA) calling the adverts "outrageous and insulting" further they wrote, "while we recognize the motivations behind the ad campaign, we are strongly opposed to the messaging.... this outrageous and insulting message could harm the Israel-Diaspora relationship."

*

The question of culture

In the late 1980s a common saying in Russia was that a person who smiles a lot is either a fool or an American. During most of the twentieth century, this would not have faced much opposition. But in 1991, two years after the fall of the Berlin Wall, McDonalds made the decision to enter Russia. They found that this saying and the notion that one shouldn't smile may pose a problem for customer service. In the midst of its preparation for the grand opening of the Moscow Pushkin Square branch of the restaurant, the first branch ever to open in Russia, McDonalds sent many of its new employees to Canada for training. During this training, McDonalds taught its new employees to prepare a burger, manage a register, deal with customers and seem cheerful and smile. McDonalds tried to teach its employees that smiling often was not only allowed, but desirable.

From individuals' humankind formed tribes, from tribes it created societies, and from societies, it created rules. These rules define what is acceptable and what is desirable within a given culture (for example - smile). In the days of old, each tribe moved to a different place. Some moved north to Europe, some traveled east, all the way to Asia. Each tribe faced different challenges, and the way in which the different tribes dealt with these challenges defined their versions of these rules. Each challenge that they overcame customized that tribe's beliefs about how the world works and why. These beliefs are subjective truths. One good way of understanding the rules and beliefs of a given culture is to think about its stories and sayings such as the Russian saying, which has an historical meaning and defines the culture.

Seeking to understand how these cultural norms come to life and the role they play in business decisions, I turned to Dr. Devout Pattanaik, an Indian with a round face and a unique ability to deliver a lecture without ever pausing his infectious smile. He is a physician by education, but his career has led him to the most unusual position—Chief Belief Officer of Future Group,

India's largest retailer. After fourteen years of experience in the pharmaceutical industry, he says that he looks at both business and modern life through the lens of mythology. By thinking about the stories told in mythology, he tries to understand cultures and the beliefs that they hold. For Dr. Pattanaik, mythology does not necessarily need to involve gods and wars of old, but can include any truths that we create for ourselves that are based on our experiences, expectations, and perceptions. These stories are the foundation of all cultures. According to Dr. Pattanaik, any attributes given to individuals are the result of a belief system within a given culture. These beliefs are subjective truths and, in general, people believe the notion that "my truth is always better than your truth."

*

I used to live on Rothschild Boulevard in Tel-Aviv. I loved living there. Walking south to north on the boulevard, I would pass the first two houses ever built in Tel-Aviv. Then, on the right, the house in which the Israeli Declaration of Independence was signed. Walking further, I'd pass a series of buildings inhabited by some of the most well-known venture capital firms in Israel and In between a series of cafés that are filled with entrepreneurs glued to their laptops.

For me Rothschild Boulevard represents not only the history of Israel, but also its future. It is a future of innovation, and it represents a journey from the past to the present. It is a journey filled with the tales told by the buildings on the boulevard. These stories are the foundation of a culture of entrepreneurship with unique characteristics, formed over the past century.

Many of the stories that originated from this boulevard can help us define Israeli culture. These stories are taught in schools and on tours; the greatest stories and the most influential ones, can be told and summarized in catch phrases. Some of these slogans have detached themselves from their original form in order to reappear in new stories that are told. Conducting many interviews, three such phrases or terms always seemed to come up. The first term is 'Haval al hazman', a Hebrew term, which can be translated, as 'a waste of time.' In Israel, this term is used so often that it has become an abbreviation (HVLAZ) as well as an adjective with both positive and negative connotations (which can be understood only by paying attention to the intonation of the speaker). The second term is 'few against many,' and the last is 'chutzpa', probably the most famous Hebrew/Yiddish term known outside of Israel.

Haval al Hazman

The term Haval al Hazman has two meanings in modern Hebrew, the first of which is positive. When one asks about a party, movie, or event, one can respond that it was 'Haval al Hazman.' This indicates that it was awesome. The second meaning is negative, and true to its literal translation- a waste of time. For example, one could say that a meeting was 'Haval al Hazman,' indicating either that it was boring or that it was great and productive. How do Israelis distinguish between these two connotations? Usually, the tone of voice determines the meaning.

It is more interesting for our purposes, however, to understand how this term came about. The term originated in the days prior to the Second World War.

Up until this time, the 'Yashuv', the early Jewish settlements in Palestine, had attempted to build a new society. Not a state, but a new type of society, one that would serve as a model for the world. They wanted to create a model in which the individual would be able to fulfill his full potential, while still being equal and working towards a common goal. As the settlements grew in land and operations, so did its need for new people. The Yashuv would not accept just anyone, as this was to be the beginning of a new society, only the best would be fit to be among its founders. The rise of the Nazi party in Germany quickly changed the Yashuv plans. Overnight, their mission moved from building a model society to providing a home and refuge to their fellow Jews fleeing Europe. These European Jews could not wait until the Yashuv finished building this home. As new immigrants from Europe flooded to Palestine, they were directed immediately to camps in order to build the new state and defend it. The story tells us that as soon as these refugees reached the shores of Palestine, they were given a shovel, and a gun, and were pushed to shore rather than slowly disembarking their ship because 'time is a horrible thing to waste' - Haval al Hazman.

Few against many

The concept of 'few against many' is rooted deep into both Israeli society and Jewish history. It is a reoccurring theme in many Israeli stories. Most of these stories are of battles and wars, they might be as old as the story of the biblical, Joshua, who led the Jewish conquest of Canaan (the biblical name of Palestine), or as new as the story of the War of Independence or that of the 1973 Yom Kippur War. The reoccurring theme is of a small fighting force that is successful when competing against a force two or three times its size. The notion of few against many is a feeling that many Israelis carry not only in military understanding, but also in the way that they conduct business. The Israeli businessman feels that he needs to prove that his company, though smaller than other players, is capable because of better resource allocation, time management, and pure wits. Remembering that, for him, time is a horrible thing to waste.

Chutzpa

The term Chutzpa has been used in past to describe the

ways in which Israeli businesses conduct themselves across the globe. It has since spilled into American culture (recently with former GOP presidential hopeful Michele Bachmann accusing US President Barack Obama of "having a lot of chutzpa" with regards to government spending). The classic story of chutzpa has even been brought into the legal sphere when a young man was brought in front of a judge, accused of murdering his parents. The young man responded to the accusation by pleading for mercy on account of the fact that he is now an orphan.

Chutzpa involves changing the rules of the game when they do not serve your best interests, yet defending them furiously when they do. The term understands that the rules of society are just that—rules created by society. As such, they can be changed. Having chutzpa involves having little respect for traditional norms if they fail to serve one's best interests.

The earliest example I could find for the use of the term was in the activities of Golda Meir, the fourth Prime Minister of Israel. In 1946, as head of the political department of the Jewish Agency, Golda Meir participated in high-level, multi-party discussions. Diplomats recall that on one occasion a member from one of the Arab states was expected to follow her speech. Because she did not want him to be heard, as Golda Meir stepped down from the stage towards her table, she pretended to not feel well and fainted, causing the discussion to end and the Arab representative to remain silent. The concept of chutzpa, of changing the rules that don't suit your purposes, is also manifested in Israelis' lack of respect for hierarchy. Israelis will respect hierarchy when its suits them. For example, during negotiations, they may refer to a superior in order to achieve better outcomes using the notion "I need to be able to sell this to my boss." However, if their boss does not agree, they may sign it anyway because the rule "you're my boss and therefore I should do as you say" does not apply in cases where the rules are not in one's favor.

These three concepts, 'time is a horrible thing to waste,' 'few against many,' and 'chutzpa,' can be understood to be the basic characteristics of the Israeli entrepreneur.

Often the first thing people notice about Israelis is their

no-tie, casual approach. It is said that in Israel a man will buy a suit only once in his life and will wear it twice: the first time at his wedding and the second time at his funeral. Today, the groom would probably not even wear a suit, and open casket funerals are not custom in Israel.

The second thing people notice about Israelis is the directness of their communication. A few months after I started working for McKinsey, I participated in a meeting with a partner who provided me with feedback on some of my client work. I stepped out of that meeting feeling very good until my manger said, "Uri, let's take a walk." We went around the building, and he asked me how I thought the meeting went, to which I responded: "Very well! I still need to work on a few items, but he was very pleased." My manager started walking a bit faster while he explained that the feedback we had just received was not entirely positive, even negative in nature. I was shocked, not so much from the feedback, but by the fact that I did not understand the subtleties of a conversation in which I had just participated. In Israel, people are direct. The speaker is responsible for the listeners' understanding, so he will attempt to be as straightforward as possible. His aim will be to communicate his messages as fast and as efficiently as possible. Again, time is a horrible thing to waste.

The last thing that may shock foreigners in Israel is a complete lack of tolerance for hierarchy. I was a soldier serving in the northern part of Israel in 1998 when a general named Erez Gerstein came to talk to us. As he entered the room, we all stood, waiting for him to instruct us to sit. He took off his hat, put his rifle on the table, and sat down, signaling us to do the same. He said that he wanted to hear from us not only what we saw in terms of Hezbollah activities, the Lebanese terrorist organization against which we were fighting, but also what we thought we should do about this situation. He finished his opening remarks by saying that he wanted to hear our thinking unfiltered. “No one has a monopoly on brain and wisdom,” he said.

Twelve years later, I was in the boardroom of an Israeli telecom company, accompanying a partner from Munich to a meeting with the CEO and some of his executives. One of the low-ranking executives began to have a side conversation with the CEO. The conversation turned into a loud disagreement and then moved from English into Hebrew. I started to translate for my partner, but I began to paraphrase when expressions involving the men's two mothers surfaced. Two years later, this low-ranking executive became the senior deputy to this same CEO.

When Cultures Clash

It will come as little surprise that different people see things differently. A story passed on in one corner of the Earth is perceived differently when it is told elsewhere. Stories are also structured differently in different places. Stories in Africa have different heroes from those told in North America. Because different people have different stories, their views of the world, of how it works and why it works the way it does, differ. These different views are the origin of inevitable misunderstandings and clashes.

Dr. Pattanaik tells a story that illustrates these differences. Alexander was a young Macedonian tutored by Aristotle until the age of sixteen. When Alexander was ten years old, a merchant presented a horse to his father, Philip II of Macedon. The horse was stubborn and wild and the servants were not able to tame him. Seeing the fear in the horse's eyes, Alexander requested to take him. He was eventually able to tame him. Philip kissed his son and declared, "My boy you must find a kingdom large enough for your ambitions!" Years later, Alexander was leading an army of 50,000 strong, seeking to reach the "ends of the world and the great outer sea." This journey brought him to the banks of the river Indus. On the banks of this river he met a gymnosophist, a monk who was staring at the sky. Alexander asked the monk what he was doing, to which the monk replied, "I am experiencing nothingness." "And what are you doing?" asked the monk of Alexander. "I am on my way to conquer the world," replied the great warrior. The two men stared at each other thinking, what a strange and pointless thing this other man is trying to do!

Two and a half thousand years later, the Israeli entrepreneur finds himself in a similar situation. Israeli culture is unique in the way that it encourages out-of-the-box thinking and the defiance of hierarchy and normal procedures. These attitudes can be a great asset, but if they are not properly understood, they can sabotage successful businesses. For the Israeli entrepreneur the notion of a long process, of dealing with hierarchy and protocol, is a waste of time. For him time is a horrible thing to waste. When he looks at the way that people conduct themselves and he finds that the rules leave him in an inferior position, he asks himself, "why not change the rules?" And when faced with resistance to such changes from multiple stakeholders, he may feel that he is indeed the 'few against many'. These feelings, which are often accompanied by strong personalities, are bound to create conflict.

To understand how to avoid these conflicts and be able to work together, I turned to the most successful and culturally diverse location - the Adlon hotel in Berlin. For over a century, this hotel has housed some of the world's greatest leaders of business and government. On any given day, its guests are composed of over twenty-five different nationalities, each with different needs and expectations. Its staff of over four hundred people is composed of an equally diverse population. The manager of this hotel is Franck Droin, a man who has lived in six countries, including Abu-Dhabi, Jordan, and Switzerland. Describing the apparent nature of his industry, Franck says that his business is about "working on the emotions of people." When he trains his employees, he explains that there is no guidebook, standard, or step framework on which one can rely. From the manager to the desk clerk, everyone needs to practice high levels of emotional intelligence.

Developing this intelligence is no easy task. In the hotel industry, high-level managers are able to develop such intelligence by working and living in different countries. By being exposed to different cultures, they understand that the ways in which they were brought up, and their beliefs about how things should work, are not necessarily global norms. This experience allows them to understand that their own belief systems are subjective and that others think differently. This understanding allows them to grow emotionally and to connect to people on a personal level. The main challenge that the industry is facing is how to provide its more junior employees with the same level of emotional intelligence as the managers, who have lived in different countries and experienced different cultures. The way Adlon trains its employees in this field is truly innovative.

The hotel has developed the notion that by encouraging its employees to participate in social and corporate responsibility programs they will develop their personal emotional intelligence. Franck and his fellow managers hold the idea that, by interacting with the less fortunate, their employees will also develop the ability to interact and connect with their more privileged guests.

By developing emotional intelligence, governments can help their populations to understand that the experience of living in different countries is an important one for successful managers. Programs such as The Erasmus Programme (European Community Action Scheme for the Mobility of University Students) and the US Peace Corps provide these benefits to their population. In addition, governments around the world can help their populations to migrate to different countries by working to lift visa restrictions and by supporting local expat populations. These experiences are vital for the global executive and worker in the international environment.

Final thoughts

We prefer to view the history of the world in chapters, as if we were participating in a great story that is being written and stored for future generations. We often look at events and try to mark their beginning, middle, and end, as if life must follow the same rules that are followed by books and plays (so said Jean-Luc Godard). The story of economic development follows different rules. There is no guarantee that the hero who rose from poverty, struggled, and succeeded will keep his might until the very end. In the world in which we live, there are numerous examples of nations who at one point were strong economic powers and at another point descended from this greatness to experience difficult times.

Japan's economy used to be a remarkable story of growth. Throughout the 1960s and 1970s, Japan was the world's second largest economy. In the decade that followed, it started an expansion period during which it more than doubled its GDP per capita. Japan was praised for its economic performance and Japanese companies were synonymous with technological innovation. By the end of the 1980s, Japanese companies were conducting massive mergers and acquisitions in the US and other heavily developed parts of the world. In 1987, *The Economist* wrote that 'the Japanese have stolen the icing'—a reference to its possession of eleven percent of world trade (just two percent behind the US that year). Despite this success, bubbles in parts of the Japanese economy (e.g., real estate) and falls in investments and levels of innovation contributed to the country's fall. Economic policies, that once fostered growth, grew irrelevant and now produced a stagnated economy. At the end of the 1990s, the term 'the lost decade' came to life. It signaled the brief period of Japanese economic stagnation. In the midst of 2005, the term was changed to 'the lost years' in order to include the decade that followed. The Japanese story shows that there is no guarantee that economies will continue to grow. It shows that the power of nations on the global stage is bound to change.

The Israeli story is a remarkable one. Israel came to life out of the wreckage of the Second World War and fought for its survival in numerous wars. Despite its security and economic condition, it welcomed massive immigration from the four corners of the earth. It went through periods of hyperinflation and sluggish growth. Yet in fifty years Israel had risen to become a hub of technological innovation. Its companies have developed voice mail, an ingestible video camera that fits inside a pill, the USB stick, and many more important and ubiquitous products. Israel is home to R&D centers for the largest companies in the world, including Microsoft, Google, Intel, Motorola, and Cisco. Its population produces more scientific papers per capita that lead to more patents per capita than any other country in the world. Still, like Japan, its past successes do not secure future rewards.

In the summer of 2011, my beloved Rothschild Boulevard, which had housed all of the struggles of the State of Israel from its Declaration of Independence to its high-tech entrepreneurs, began to house a new struggle, this time for social justice. Thousands of protesters occupied the boulevard with tents, feeling that the prices of everything from basic food to housing had risen at a pace that did not match citizens' income levels. Ten years after the dynamic growth of the 1990s and the promises that followed, too many felt that the promises of a better life and a more just society were simply not being fulfilled. The rising costs of living, alongside stagnant wages, have left many feeling that prosperity has passed them by. For all of the challenges that the state has overcome, the protesters felt that Israel's biggest challenges are still ahead and need to be addressed. During that summer, these protesters talked about the cost of living, but also about social inequality. The gap between the haves and the have-nots has been widening to frightening levels. This gap, which had once seemed easy to overcome, had become so wide that a structural change is needed. The level of education of some sectors of the population has made it impossible for graduates to move into the middle class. In one of the speeches delivered at the main square, a leader of the protesters claimed, "Once entrepreneurial spirit entailed that all is possible. If you have a good idea and the energy to match you would succeed. Today the spirit has turned to despair."

The rhetoric of the demonstrations of the summer of 2011 may have been harsh, but it was a true reflection of the state of mind that people possess after years of slow growth that was eventually toppled by a financial crisis.

Although some think of Israel as a small country surrounded by enemies, in the world economy it is not an island. As the last crisis has proved, the challenges ahead that face the rest of the world will also directly and indirectly affect the Israeli economy and its prospects for growth. A decline in available capital for investments will affect the ability of companies within Israel, big and small, to raise funds. Demographic changes in the US and Europe will affect spending patterns and as such, the availability of customers for Israeli companies in these markets. A rise in energy prices will affect both production and transportation costs, making it ever more difficult for these companies to compete against companies that originate from more labor-intensive economies. A rise in food prices and the scarcity of other resources may lead to higher inflation levels or to a lower currency exchange rate that will harm the competitiveness of Israeli companies. And changes in technology will affect the pace and direction of innovation, making countries with available technological skills ever more attractive to international businesses.

Israel can overcome these challenges. It can act and innovate its way into growth, but… It can seize these challenges and pioneer new scientific discoveries and make technological breakthroughs, but -there is always a huge *but*. To succeed, Israel must understand that the origins of the next wave of innovation will be different to the ones it tapped into during the 1980s and 1990s. The sources of past innovations were mainly military driven, and the intersection between different segments and industries that are active in Israel may not necessarily be relevant to the next problems that face the world.

In order to stay at the center of innovation, Israel first needs to move closer to its customers and closer to global markets. This can only be accomplished through a series of investments and activities that will allow Israeli companies to compete and interact with customers more directly and build relationships with them in more profound ways. To ensure that the Israeli economy is ever more integrated into the world economy, the government should start by easing access to customers. It is the role of the Israeli government to secure capital for organizations as well as the best and brightest talent in order to allow these companies to be competitive once they arrive at global markets. By reducing these barriers, the government can allow companies to focus on what they are good at—innovation.

There is an old joke that says that every country is hoping for a miracle, but Israel is the only one that makes its decisions by relying on one. The miracle of Israel already happened a long time ago, and what comes next has nothing to do with chance. It has everything to do with innovation.

Epilogue – Innovation is in desperate need of some innovation

For about a decade, managers have been devoting more and more time and resources to the topic of innovation. This surge has resulted in new roles such as "innovation manager," and new realms and endeavours like "innovation strategy." The hype has also found its way into the academic world, with new courses and even degrees offered in Innovation (for example City University London), and peaked in US President Barack Obama's 2nd State of the Union Address, in which he used the word innovation 11 times.

Despite a growing amount of resources devoted to innovation, more and more evidence suggests a disconnect between the efforts to spur innovation and actual results. When examining both companies' performance and macroeconomic data (in Europe and the US) there is little to suggest any substantial innovative activity is taking place . Economists like Tyler Cowen have named this era "the great stagnation." The board of directors of the hallmark of innovation – Apple – are reportedly concerned about "the company's pace of innovation," as it hasn't introduced a game-changing product since the iPad in early 2010.

So how is it that despite all of these efforts, companies across the board are failing to meet their innovation goals? For two reasons: Managers are, first, confusing innovation and creativity, and second, restricting innovative activities by focusing resources on incremental improvements.

It is understood that creativity plays a role in the innovative process, but where does one end the other begin? Creativity is the process of inventing new things, new models, products and services; innovation is something much bigger. Innovation is a paradigm shift in which we change the means by which value is created in a product.

Take a look at your phone for example. Ten years ago, Nokia and Motorola were the dominant players in the mobile phone industry. Each year they would introduce devices that were smaller, had better connectivity and more features. In June, 2007, however, Apple didn't just introduce a better phone – the iPhone was something else entirely. Its main focus was not to make phone calls but to stay connected. Six years later, phones are devices that also make phone calls – though if "calls" was an app, it probably wouldn't even be the most-used.

But innovation does more than just change the value of a product – it disrupts the value chain. The travel industry is no stranger to such disruption. In 1996, a Microsoft spin-off by the name of Expedia.com offered users the option of booking their own flights online. Over the next 15 years, the company single-handedly made more and more travel agents redundant by offering customers more travel information and options than the traditional channels. Expedia thus changed the entire industry value chain, forcing airlines and hotels alike to change the way they service and price their products.

In 2008, another innovation changed the travel industry – Airbnb launched, offering a digital platform to rent rooms and apartments for short-term stays. This year, some nine million people stayed in an Airbnb location across 192 countries. The company did more than just disrupt the hospitality business – its model (along with other collaborative consumption efforts such as RelayRides and Costockage, which allows other people to rent your car or storage area) led the way to the creation of the "shared economy" in which people rent beds, storage space, boats and other assets directly from each other, co-ordinating over the internet.

Creativity was indeed present at Apple, Expedia and Airbnb in these cases, but it was only by taking the process to the next level that their creations became innovations. Their products and services challenged previous conventions; they changed the process by which value is created and in doing so, changed the way we viewed the product.

By attributing the word 'innovation' to creative products and services, managers are stripping away the meaning that the term once held. Words and nuance matter. Creativity provides companies with tactical gains. While new products might allow for increase in market share and allow companies to better service their customers, companies can't expect to make huge leaps forward by settling for creativity alone.

Indeed, innovation itself is in desperate need of some innovation. The solution to this stagnation is not to put more resources into innovation, but rather to create a new paradigm. One that is not concerned with finding new solutions to old problems. This new paradigm must be concerned with finding new problems and addressing them in creative ways. To make this shift, organizations need to change their focus from short to long term benefits and change to the way they manage risk.

The process of creating a transformational change requires substantial resources over time, to create the basis for a sustainable business. Building foundations rarely produces immediate results but when put together properly, it can create much larger gains in the long run. Take the pharmaceutical industry as an example. Viagra was one of Pfizer's most innovative products, protected with over 100 patents and generating over $25 billion since its introduction in 1998. But its success did not come overnight – in fact, analysts initially questioned whether the blue pill was worth the marketing budget and other resources it was assigned. It took the company four long years to convince patients to ask for and doctors to subscribe the drug – and the rest is history.

The pharmaceutical industry can also teach us about best practices for innovation risk management. Innovative companies manage their products and initiatives as a portfolio. In such a portfolio some products contain low risk while other have a large probability to fail. Managing the risk from a portfolio perspective and not the individual project allows taking the risk bias away from the equation. As such, this type of practice allows for proper funding of innovative – though potentially risky – initiatives. By properly funding each initiative, these companies truly commit to their development, understanding that innovation arises through a long process of trial-and-error. It's easy to question development and ideas, but only by truly committing to a project can its potential be realized.

The use and misuse of the word "innovative" is bringing new voices that try to abolish the word from the business lexicon (e.g., Bill Taylor, Stop me before I "innovate" again, HBR). Doing so would be dangerous and irresponsible. Instead, managers should attribute words correctly and innovate the way they innovate.

Sources

Angel, Dan & Connelly T. Riptide: The New Normal for Higher Education. The Publishing Place, New York, 2011.

Anthony H. Cordesman and Arleigh A. Burke. Saudi Arabia enters into the 21 century. Center for Strategic and International Studies (CSIS). Washington, 2002.

Atkins, Charles and Susan Lund "The economic Impact of increase US savings" McKinsey on Finance Number 31, 2009.

Avishai, Bernard. "Israel Future: Brainpower, High Tech, and Peace" Harverd Business Review, November 1991.

Bates, Thomas W, Kathleen M Kajle and Rene M Sultz "Why do US firms hold so much more cash then they used to?", the journal of finance, Volume 64, Number 5, 2009.

Bell Katherine. "Investing in Infrastructure Means Investing in Innovation". Harverd Business Review Blog. March 15, 2012.

Beinhoker, Eric, Diana Farrell, and Ezra Greenberg, "Why Baby Boomers Will Need to Work Longer," McKinsey Quarterly, November 2008.

Ben-Porath, Yoram. The Israeli Economy: Maturing Through Crises. Cambridge: Harverd University Press, 1986.

Bill Lewis, Diana Farrell, Mike Nevens, Lenny Mendonca, Vincent Palmade, Greg Hughes, James Manyika, Heino Fabender, Eric Labaye, Shyam Lal, Roger Roberts. Whatever happened to the new economy?. McKinsey Global Institute. November 2011.

Brian M Riedl. Why Government Spending Does Not Stimulate Economic Growth: Answering the Critics And how taxes affect economic growth. Wall Street Journal, January 8, 2010.

"Can it get worse?", the economist, Sep 10, 2011.

Charles Leadbeater: Education innovation in the slums, Ted, June 2010.

Charles Roxburgh, James Manyika, Richard Dobbs and Jan Mischkeɣ Trading myths: Addressing misconceptions about trade, jobs, and competitiveness. McKinsey Global Institute, May 2012.

Cooper, Richard N, "Living with Global Imbalance"

Brooking Papers on Economic Activity, Number 2, 2007.

Cooper, Richard N, “Global Imbalance: Globalization, demography and sustainability” Journal of Economic Perspective, Volume 22, Number 3, 2008.

Corneo, Giacomo, Matthias Keese and Carsten Schroder. “The Effect of Saving Subsidies on Household Saving: Evidence from Germany”, Discussion paper 3, Free University Berlin, school of Business & Economics, 2010.

Congressional Budget Office (CBO), The Long Term Budget Outlook, June 2010.

David, Anthony, The Sky Is the Limit: Al Shimmer, the founder of the Israeli Aircraft Industry. (In Hebrew) Tel Aviv: Schocken Books, 2008.

Diana Farrell, Diana Farell and Ezra Greenberg, “The economic Impacy of an aging Japan” McKinsey Quarterly, May 2005.

Dobbs R, Oppenheim J, Thompson F, Brinkman M, Zornes .Resource revolution: Meeting the world’s energy, materials, food, and water needs. McKinsey & Company, November 2011.

Doing business report, World Bank http://www.doingbusiness.org/data/exploreeconomies/saudi-arabia/

Lenny Mendonca, Mike Nevens, James Manyika, Shyam Lal, Roger Roberts, Martin Baily, Terra Terwilliger, Allen Webb, Anil Kale, Mukund Ramaratnam, Eva Rzepniewski, Nick Santhanam, Mike Cho. How IT enables productivity growth. McKinsey Global Institute. May 2002.

"Facing Tomorrow", Session at the Israeli Presidential Conference, Jerusalem, May 2008.

Frieda, Robert, and Paul Israel. 1986. *Edison's electric light: biography of an* invention. New Brunswick, New Jersey: Rutgers University Press. pages 115–117.

Friedman, Thomas L. The World Is Flat: A brief History of the Twenty- First Century. New-York: Farrar, Straus and Giroux, 2005.

Friedman, Thomas L. That Used to Be Us: How America Fell Behind in the World It Invented and How

We Can Come Back. New-York: Farrar, Straus and Giroux, 2011.

George Stalk Jar." The Threat of Global Gridlock,", Harvard Business Review, July 2009.

"High stakes battle brews at Ashdod port", Haaretz, November 16, 2011.

IMD World Competitiveness Yearbook. Lausanne, Switzerland: IMD, 2007.

IMD World Competitiveness Yearbook. Lausanne, Switzerland: IMD, 2008.

IMD World Competitiveness Yearbook. Lausanne, Switzerland: IMD, 2009.

IMD World Competitiveness Yearbook. Lausanne, Switzerland: IMD, 2010.

IMD World Competitiveness Yearbook. Lausanne, Switzerland: IMD, 2011.

James Gwartney, Robert Lawson & Joshua Hall. Economic Freedom of the world 2011 annual report, Fraser Institute 2012.

Joel Klein, Michelle Rhee, Peter C. Gorman, Ron Huberman, Carol R. Johnson, Andrés A. Alonso, Tom Boasberg, Arlene C. Ackerman, William R. Hite Jr., Jean-Claude Brizard, José M. Torres, J. Wm. Covington, Terry B. Grier, Paul Vallas, Eugene White, LaVonne Sheffield. "How to fix our schools: A manifesto". The Washington post, October 10, 2010.

John Battelle. The Search: How Google and Its Rivals Rewrote the Rules of Business and Transformed Our Culture. Penguin, New York, 2005.

Joyner, Christopher. In Boycott and Blacklist: A History of Arab Economic Warfare Against Israel, edited by Aaron J. Sarna. Lanham, Md. Rowman & Littlefield 1986.

Josh Lerner The boulevard of broken dreams: Why Public Efforts to Boost Entrepreneurship and Venture Capital Have Failed--and What to Do About It (Kauffman Foundation Series on Innovation and Entrepreneurship). Princeton University Press. September 28, 2009.

Kao, John. Innovation Nation: How America Is Losing

Its Innovation Edge, Why It Matters and What Can We Do to Get It Back. New York: Free Press, 2007.

Khanna, Raun, and Krishna G. Palepu. "Emerging Giants: Building World-Class Companies in Developing Countries" Harverd Business Review, October 2006.

Lifschitz , R. "Going Civilian: Benny Levin - Nice Systems" (In Hebrew), Globes, 26 December 99.

Louise Wilkinson. "Engineering Brain Drain?" Boing: Frontier, December 2007.

Matthieu Pélissié du Rausas, James Manyika, Eric Hazan, Jacques Bughin, Michael Chui, Rémi Said. Internet matters: The Net's sweeping impact on growth, jobs, and prosperity. McKinsey Global Institute. May 2011.

Mark W. Johnson and Josh Suskewicz. How to Jump-Start the Clean-Tech Economy, Harvard business review, November 2009.

New Zealand Business & Investment Opportunities Yearbook, International Business Publications, USA;

3rd edition. January 1, 2009.

OECD Investment policy review: Israel 2002, OECD, September 16, 2002.

OECD Economic Surveys: Israel 2011, OECD, January 11, 2012.

Peter Bisson, Elizabeth Stephenson, and S. Patrick Viguerie. "Global forces: an introduction" McKinsey Quarterly, June 2010.

Prestowitz Clyde. Three Billion New Capitalists: The Great Shift of Wealth and Power to the East. Basic Books. New York, 2005.

Reinhart, Carmen and Kenneth Rogoff. This Time It's Different: Eight Centuries of Financial Folly. Princeton, 2009.

Richard Dobbs, Jeremy Oppenheim, Fraser Thompson, Marcel Brinkman, Marc Zornes. Resource revolution: Meeting the world's energy, materials, food, and water needs. McKinsey Global Institute, November 2011.

Richard Dobbs, Susan Lund, Charles Roxburgh, James Manyika, Alex Kim, Andreas Schreiner, Riccardo Boin, Rohit Chopra, Sebastian Jauch, Hyun Kim, Megan McDonald, John Piotrowski .Farewell to cheap capital? The implications of long term shifts in global investment and saving, McKinsey Global Institute, December 2010.

Roger Abravanel. The promised economy, McKinsey Quarterly, November 2001.

Sergio Sandoval and Robin Nuttal "The new value at stake from regulation, McKinsey Quarterly, Jan 2010.

Scott C. Beardsley and Diana Farrell. "Regulation that's good for competition" McKinsey Quarterly, May 2005.

"Small is not beautiful", The Economist ,March 3, 2012.

Tabarrok, Alex, Launching the Innovation Renaissance: A new path to bring smart ideas to the market, Ted, 2011.

Tony Long .If the Check Says 'Google Inc.,' We're 'Google Inc.'. Wired Magazine Sep 2007.

"Talent Shortage Survey results 2011". Manpower 2012 available at http://us.manpower.com/us/en/multimedia/2011-Talent-Shortage-Survey.pdf

Thomas A. Kochan “A Jobs Compact for America's Future” , Harverd Business Review, March 2012.

World Bank, Transition – The First Ten Years: Analysis and Lessons for Eastern Europe and the Former Soviet Union, Washington: World Bank, 2002.

World Economic Forum, The Global Competitiveness Report, 2010.

“What next for the startup nation”, The Economist. January 21, 2012.

Wildavsky, B. The Great Brain Race: How Global Universities Are Reshaping the World. Princeton University Press; Boston, 2010.

Zohar Blumenkrantz .“Turkey restricts use of airspace by Israeli cargo planes,” Haaretz, Feb 26, 2012.

On Line resources:

Bank of International Settlements: http://www.bis.org/

Bank of Israel: http://www.bankisrael.gov.il/firsteng.htm

Bloomberg: http://www.bloomberg.com/markets/

Eurostat, European statistic:
http://epp.eurostat.ec.europa.eu/portal/page/portal/euro

stat/home/

Haver Analytics: http://www.haver.com/

HIS Global Insight: http://www.ihs.com/products/global-insight/index.aspx

International Monetary Fund: http://www.imf.org/external/index.htm

Israel bureau of statistics: http://www1.cbs.gov.il/reader/cw_usr_view_Folder?ID=141

IVS research center: http://www.ivc-online.com/

NASDAQ Stock Market: http://www.nasdaq.com/

OECD. StatExtracts: http://stats.oecd.org/

Oxford Economics: http://www.oxfordeconomics.com/OE_FA_MODS.asp

Tel-Aviv Stock Exchange: http://www.tase.co.il/TASEEng/

The World Bank: http://data.worldbank.org/

TurkStat: Turkish Statistical Institute: http://www.turkstat.gov.tr/

UN Comtrade: http://comtrade.un.org/

United Nations Statistics Division:

http://unstats.un.org/unsd/demographic/sconcerns/default.htm

UN population database:
http://esa.un.org/unpd/wpp/unpp/panel_population.htm

ViewsWire · Economist Intelligence Unit:
http://viewswire.eiu.com/index.asp

CPSIA information can be obtained
at www.ICGtesting.com
Printed in the USA
LVHW03s2336251018
594897LV00002B/234/P